MORAVIAN DAILY TEXTS

Bible Texts with Hymn Verses and Prayers for Every Day in the Year

2023

Two Hundred Ninety-Third Year

The Moravian Church in America
1021 Center St., Bethlehem, PA 18018
459 S. Church St., Winston-Salem, NC 27101
www.moravian.org

Moravian Daily Texts 2023

Verse translation by Erdmute Frank. Compilation and copy editing by Susan Kiefner, with assistance from Mike Riess and Jill Bruckart.

On this year's cover: Handmade stained glass Moravian stars. Photo by Mike Riess, IBOC.

Book design: Sandy Fay, Laughing Horse Graphics, Inc., Doylestown, Pa.

Printed by McNaughton & Gunn, Inc., Saline, Mich.

Printed in the United States of America

ISBN: 978-1-954549-05-0 paperback edition

INTERPROVINCIAL BOARD OF COMMUNICATION

Moravian Daily Texts 2023

Friedrich Reinhardt Verlag, Lörrach/Basel, 2022

Druck: Gustav Winter,
Druckerei und Verlagsgesellschaft mbH, Herrnhut

ISBN: 978-3-7245-2557-8

NEW EVERY MORNING

"The steadfast love of the Lord never ceases, his mercies never come to an end; they are new every morning."
Lamentations 3:22,23

The first printed edition of the *Daily Texts* (Losungen) was published in Herrnhut, Saxony, in 1731. The title page of that edition quoted the passage from Lamentations and promised a daily message from God that would be new every morning. It was an outgrowth of a spiritual renewal of the Moravian Church (Unitas Fratrum) that dated from August 13, 1727.

In 1722 refugees from Bohemia and Moravia began arriving at the estate of Count Nicholas Ludwig von Zinzendorf (1700-1760), where he gave them a welcome and land on which to establish the settlement of Herrnhut ("Watch of the Lord").

Each day the settlers came together for morning and evening devotions, consciously placing their lives in the context of God's Word. On May 3, 1728, during the evening service, Count Zinzendorf gave the congregation a "watchword" for the next day. It was to be a "Losung" (watchword) to accompany them through the whole day.

Thereafter one or more persons of the congregation went daily to each of the 32 houses in Herrnhut to bring them the watchword for the day, and engage the families in pastoral conversations about the text.

From this oral tradition, the *Daily Texts* soon became fixed in printed form. Zinzendorf compiled 365 watchwords for the year and the first edition of the Losungen was published for 1731.

Even in the first editions there appeared the characteristic coupling of a Bible verse and hymn stanza. Zinzendorf called the hymns "collects" and considered them to be the answer of the congregation to the Word of God. The *Daily Texts* would be a great deal poorer without the mixture of God's Word and our human response.

The watchword soon became accompanied by a "doctrinal" text. The idea of an additional text grew out of a number of collections of texts from the Bible that were put together by Zinzendorf. Such additional lists (some of them for children) were used for special study within the groups in the community, and they came to be referred to as doctrinal texts.

For the *Daily Texts,* as for the whole Moravian Church, Count Zinzendorf's death (May 9, 1760), was a turning point.

His co-workers sensed the uniqueness of Zinzendorf's watchwords, textbooks, and lessons and had them published at Barby-on-the-Elbe in a four-volume collection 1762.

From then on the watchwords and doctrinal texts are distinguished by the way they are selected each year. The watchwords are chosen from various verse collections and, since 1788, they have been drawn by lot from a collection of around 2,000 suitable Old Testament texts. The doctrinal texts are not chosen by lot but are selected. The difference between the watchwords and doctrinal texts was explained in 1801 as follows: "The watchword is either a promise, an encouragement, an admonition or word of comfort; the doctrinal text contains a point of revealed doctrine."

By 1812 it was established that all watchwords would be drawn by lot from a selection of Old Testament texts, and the doctrinal texts would be selected from the New Testament. No doctrinal text is used more than once in a given year. By the end of the nineteenth century, the custom was established to relate the two texts in theme or thought.

Into all the world

Another characteristic of the *Daily Texts* that was already apparent in the early years of its publication was its worldwide distribution. Missionaries who went as "messengers" from Herrnhut after 1732 had a *Daily Texts (Losungen)* in their luggage. They felt united with their home congregation through the daily contemplation of the same Scripture passages.

The *Daily Texts* of 1739 lists a multitude of places around the globe where messengers were witnessing for the Savior. The introduction read:

> "The Good Word of the Lord, 1739, From all the Prophets for His congregations, and servants at Herrnhut, Herrnhaag, Herrendijk [Holland], Pilgerruh [Denmark], Ebersdof, Jena, Amsterdam, Rotterdam, London, Oxford, Berlin, Greenland, St. Croix, St. John and St. Thomas [Virgin Islands], Berbice [Guyana], Palestine, Surinam, Savannah in Georgia, among the Moors in Carolina, with the wild Indians in Irene

> [an island in the Savannah River in Georgia], in Pennsylvania, among the Hottentots [South Africa], in Guinea, in Latvia, Estonia and Lithuania, Russia, on the White Sea, in Lappland, Norway, in Switzerland, [Isle of] Man, Hittland [Scotland], in prison, on pilgrimage, to Ceylon, Ethiopia, Persia, on visitation to the missionaries among the heathen, and elsewhere on land and sea."

This distribution of the Moravians into every continent in the known world seems all the more amazing when you consider that the settlement at Herrnhut was only 17 years old, and the first missionaries had gone out only seven years earlier in 1732.

Present membership of the worldwide Moravian Church is more than 1 million in 21 provinces. The *Daily Texts* has a press run of more than 1 million copies in the German language alone. This far surpasses the 25,000 members of the Moravian Church in all of Europe. Other language editions bring the total circulation of this small devotional book to over 1.5 million copies. The *Daily Texts* is now published in more than 50 languages and dialects.

The physical form of the *Daily Texts* varies considerably from country to country. Some, like this North American edition, have a separate page for the verses, hymns, and prayers of each day. Others have several days' texts printed on one page, which makes a thin, pocket-size volume. Some are beautiful examples of the printing and bookbinding arts. Others are simply photocopied and stapled together.

These external nonessentials pale beside the fact that this little book is probably the most widely read devotional guide in the world, next to the Bible. It forms an invisible bond between Christians on all continents, transcending barriers of confession, race, language, and politics. In its quiet way it performs a truly ecumenical service for the whole of Christendom.

North American editions

The printing of the *Daily Texts* in North America dates back at least to 1767, when the Losungen was printed "at Bethlehem on the Forks of the Delaware by Johan Brandmuller." The printer's imprint bears the date of 1767 as well and may have been an extra printing for the German version done at Barby-on-the-Elbe in Germany, where most of the printing was done for the Moravian Church those days.

During the crucial days of the Revolution, the German-language edition was printed in Philadelphia by Heinrich Miller, who had worked for Benjamin Franklin when he first came to America. The daily text for July 4, 1776, was from Isaiah 55:5—"Behold, you shall call nations that you know not, and nations that knew you not shall run to you" (RSV).

English versions were printed in London as early as 1746, and the title page bears the imprint of "James Hutton near the Golden Lion in Fetter Lane." Hutton was the well-known London printer associated with the Moravian Church who was a friend of John and Charles Wesley in the formative years of their ministry.

The 1850s were crucial years for the Moravian Church in America as the congregations established in the United States broke away from direct control from the Moravian headquarters in Europe. Both German and English editions of the *Daily Texts* were regularly printed in Philadelphia or Bethlehem, Pennsylvania, and in a few years the custom was established to include the statistics of the provinces and districts of the Moravian Church in America.

The biblical texts for each day are chosen in Herrnhut, Germany, and then sent around the world to those who prepare the different language editions. Since 1959 the edition published in the United States has included a prayer for each day. For this North American edition, the hymns are chosen or written, and the prayers are written by Moravian clergy and laypersons from the United States and Canada. Each month is prepared by a different individual or couple, of a variety of ages, so that the prayers reflect the great diversity of devotion in the Moravian Church. We are grateful for the work and inspired words these writers offer and their contributions strengthen each year's edition of the *Moravian Daily Texts*.

DAILY TOPICS FOR PRAYER

On August 27, 1727, certain members of the Moravian Church in Herrnhut, Saxony, formed a remarkable prayer union known as the "Hourly Intercession." This provided that, for every hour of the day and night, one of the volunteer intercessors would, for one hour in private, bear on his or her heart and mind the interests and hopes of the Kingdom of God in the world. This wonderful intercession continued for over 100 years.

On August 27, 1872, a Moravian Prayer union was formed in England as a form of resuscitation of the Hourly Intercession, and today its members are found in all areas of the Moravian world. You are invited to join in this prayer covenant. The following prayer suggestions may be helpful:

Sunday: The Church At Worship. For her purity and peace, unity and power. For the congregation to which we belong or with which we worship. For the ministry of the word of God. For the winning of people into fellowship with Christ. For all church schools, youth ministries, and other church groups at work.

Monday: The Church At Work. For the church in its mission next door and in other lands. For new congregations and specialized ministries. For the workers and leaders in these endeavors. For the worker volunteers to carry out the mission of the church.

Tuesday: Home and School. For households. For the Christian education of the young, and that our children may be led to give themselves to Christ. For all schools and teachers. For young people enrolled in colleges and universities. For the training of ministers in theological seminaries.

Wednesday: For Those In Need. For all in special need, whether as aged, sick, poor, or homeless. For those in prison. For all victims of famine, oppression, aggression, and war.

Thursday: Our Nation and Our World. For those who govern and for those who are governed. For the guidance of God to all who are in authority. For unity of nations and all agencies for peace. For the whole human family and equal rights for all. For the guidance and blessing of God as humanity enters the future.

Friday: Our Own Church Fellowship. For the purity, zeal, and practice of the church as a witnessing fellowship of the love of God. That the church may be a light to the world wherever its congregations are found, and that it may be active in redeeming mission in these communities.

Saturday: The Witness of Christians. That all who confess the name of Christ may grow in the grace and knowledge of Jesus Christ as Lord and Savior.

"O thou King of kings and Lord of lords, who desirest that all people should dwell together in unity, let thy will be known and done among the nations; guide their feet into the way of peace. Remember us and all humanity in thy mercy. Deliver us from the sins which give rise to war and conflict, and strengthen within our hearts the will to establish righteousness and justice in the earth. Give unto us and to all who worship thee the sincere desire to live in peaceful and loving fellowship with all people. Fix our minds and hearts upon thine eternal purposes for your children on earth."

— A Prayer for Peace

THE *DAILY TEXTS* IN FAMILY WORSHIP

Almost from the very beginning the *Daily Texts* has been used as a guide for family worship as well as for private and personal devotions. The use of the *Daily Texts* in family worship will vary depending on the time available and the age of the children. One of the values of the *Daily Texts* is that it is adaptable to numerous patterns of use.

One pattern followed by many families is to begin the meal (usually breakfast or the evening meal) with the reading of the texts of the day and the accompanying hymn stanzas. After this, the family joins in the blessing or table grace. A suitable blessing may be chosen from among the following:

Come, Lord Jesus, our Guest to be,
and bless these gifts bestowed by thee.
Bless thy dear ones everywhere,
and keep them in thy loving care.

Be present at our table, Lord;
be here and everywhere adored;
from thine all-bounteous hand our food
may we receive with gratitude.

The worship of the family can then close with a prayer offered in the leader's own words or in those of the printed prayer offered in the *Daily Texts.* As a part of free prayer by the leader or in connection with the printed prayer, use can be made from day to day of the subjects of the Daily Topics for Prayer as given in the preceding pages.

HOW TO USE THE *DAILY TEXTS*

The strength of the *Daily Texts* lies in presenting the Scripture unhindered by illustration. The texts are left to stand alone and to speak to each reader in his or her life. This also allows the *Daily Texts* to be adaptable to different patterns of devotion and study.

Contents For Each Day

136 MAY

1 **Tuesday, May 16** — Psalm 65:9–13
Proverbs 8:1–9:6; 1 Corinthians 14:36–15:2

2 **Some sat in darkness and in gloom, prisoners in misery and in irons. Then they cried to the Lord in their trouble, and he saved them from their distress. Let them thank the Lord for his steadfast love, for his wonderful works to humankind. Psalm 107:10,13,15**

3
> Since we, though unworthy, 746
> through electing grace,
> 'mid your ransomed people
> have obtained a place,
> Lord, may we be faithful
> to our cov'nant found,
> to you, as our shepherd,
> and your flock fast bound.

4 **Blessed are those who are persecuted for righteousness' sake, for theirs is the kingdom of heaven. Matthew 5:10**

3
> "The soul that on Jesus still leans for repose, 709
> I will not, I will not desert to its foes;
> that soul, though all hell should endeavor to shake,
> I'll never, no, never, no, never forsake!"

5 Sometimes, Lord, we forget that you are the light in the darkest nights of our souls. Sometimes, real persecution happens to people who are tortured, imprisoned, and martyred for their faith, hope, and trust in you as their guiding light. Help us to recognize the risks involved in being a Christian, and to truly be willing to sacrifice our time and energy for your cause. In the name of the one who died for us, help us live for you. Amen.

1. **SCRIPTURE LESSONS:** At the top of each page for ongoing study. Not related to the printed texts. Monday through Saturday are part of a plan to read through the Psalms in one year and the rest of the Bible in two. Sundays and special days are the assigned lessons for that day of the church year from the Moravian Revised Common Lectionary, also common to many denominations.

2. **WATCHWORD FOR THE DAY:** From the Old Testament, the first printed text. It is to be a "watchword" to accompany you throughout the day. Usually a promise, encouragement, admonition, or comfort.

3. **HYMN VERSES:** Broken down by meter and usually related to the watchword or theme for the day. It is a devotional response or commentary on the text. Can be used for prayers.

4. **DOCTRINAL TEXT:** From the New Testament. Usually contains some point of Christian doctrine to expand on the watchword.

5. **PRAYER:** A response to God of praise, confession, thanksgiving, or intercession in light of the texts and hymn verses.

- Every Sunday and some church holidays, the *Daily Texts* page will include the **WATCHWORD FOR THE WEEK/ HOLIDAY**. Like the daily watchword, the weekly/holiday text is to accompany the reader throughout the week or holiday and is related to the events of the church year. These differ every year based upon the lectionary cycle.

Devotions

The printed texts, hymn verses, and prayers are the heart of the devotional guide. Their purpose is to help the reader get more closely in touch with God and to meditate upon the Word of God. When reading the texts, hymns and prayers, feel the encouragement found in them. Hear any word or correction for your life; ponder the great message of faith; meditate upon the hymn verses and prayers; feel God's presence surrounding you in faith; and in silence, hear God's word speaking to you.

These texts can also be the center of a daily spiritual diary where you keep a journal of your daily meditations and their meaning in your life.

ACKNOWLEDGMENTS

Bible texts in this publication are quoted from the *New Revised Standard Version Bible,* © 1989 by the Division of Christian Education of the National Council of the Churches of Christ in the United States of America, and are used by permission. Verses marked NIV are taken from *The Holy Bible New International Version®,* NIV®, © 1973, 1978, 1984, 2011 by Biblica, Inc.® Used by permission. All rights reserved worldwide. Verses marked NASB and NASB1995 are taken from the *New American Standard Bible®,* © 1960, 1962, 1963, 1968, 1971, 1972, 1973, 1975, 1977, 1995 by The Lockman Foundation. Used by permission. Verses marked NKJV are taken from the *New King James Version®* © 1982 by Thomas Nelson, Inc. Used by permission. All rights reserved. Verses marked GNT are taken from the *Good News Translation,* ©1992 by the American Bible Society. Verses marked ESV are taken from The Holy Bible, English Standard Version © 2001, 2016 by Crossway, a publishing ministry of Good News Publishers. Used by permission. All rights reserved.

Sunday readings are taken from the *Revised Common Lectionary,* © 1992 by the Consultation on Common Texts (CCT).

Unless otherwise noted, hymn stanzas found in the *Daily Texts* are taken from the *Moravian Book of Worship,* 1995. The number found to the right of each stanza designates the source of the stanza in that hymnal. If the number is preceded by a p the hymn used is from one of the liturgies and the p designates the page number. The letter b after a number denotes the Hymnal and Liturgies of the Moravian Church Unitas Fratrum, 1920. The letter r after a number denotes the Hymnal of the Moravian Church, 1969. The letter s after a number denotes a hymn or song from *Sing to the Lord A New Song, A New Moravian Songbook,* 2013. The letters Si after a number denotes a hymn used is from the *Singing from the Heart, a Shorter Moravian Hymnal and Liturgies.* When hymns are copyrighted, information is given at the bottom of the page; we gratefully acknowledge permission to use copyrighted material.

Hymn stanzas are broken down by meter except when space would not allow.

The Scripture readings for Monday through Saturday are part of a plan to read through the Old and New Testaments in two years and the Psalms in one year.

First Sunday after Christmas

Watchword for the week — I will recount the gracious deeds of the Lord, the praiseworthy acts of the Lord, because of all that the Lord has done for us. Isaiah 63:7

Sunday, January 1 — Isaiah 63:7-9; Psalm 148
Hebrews 2:10-18; Matthew 2:13-23

My soul thirsts for God, for the living God. When shall I come and behold the face of God? Psalm 42:2

As the deer pants for the water, p28*
so my soul longs after you.
You alone are my heart's desire,
and I long to worship you.
You alone are my strength, my shield;
to you alone may my spirit yield.
You alone are my heart's desire,
and I long to worship you.

For everyone who asks receives, and everyone who searches finds, and for everyone who knocks, the door will be opened. Matthew 7:8

Ask and it shall be given unto you, 605**
seek and you shall find,
knock and the door shall be opened unto you—
Allelu, alleluia!

Lord, thank you for the gift of curiosity, the hunger to know more of you, and the desire to grow deeper roots into the soil of your grace and love. We ask, Lord, and you respond. Amen.

Monday, January 2 — Psalm 1
1 Chronicles 3; Acts 9:1–9

Is Ephraim my dear son? Is he the child I delight in? As often as I speak against him, I still remember him. Therefore I am deeply moved for him; I will surely have mercy on him, says the Lord. Jeremiah 31:20

Forgive me, Lord, for this I pray, 569
the wrong that I have done this day.
May peace with God and neighbor be,
before I sleep, restored to me.

God, who is rich in mercy, out of the great love with which he loved us even when we were dead through our trespasses, made us alive together with Christ. Ephesians 2:4-5

And can it be that I should gain 773
an int'rest in the Savior's blood?
Died he for me, who caused his pain—
for me, who caused his bitter death?
Amazing love! How can it be
that you, my Lord, should die for me?
Amazing love! How can it be
that you, my Lord, should die for me?

Merciful God, we are grateful for your tenderness and patience with our failures and flaws. Help us to fix our hearts on the power of your love and the transformation it brings, as we journey with our imperfections. Amen.

Tuesday, January 3 — Psalm 2
1 Chronicles 4:1–23; Acts 9:10–22

Lord, plead my cause and redeem me; revive me according to your word. Psalm 119:154 NKJV

O wind of God, come, bend us, break us, p47
till humbly we confess our need.
Then in your tenderness remake us;
revive, restore, for this we plead.

The Lord is faithful; he will strengthen you and guard you from the evil one. 2 Thessalonians 3:3

God is my strong salvation, 769
no enemy I fear;
he hears my supplication,
dispelling all my care;
if he, my head and master,
defend me from above,
what pain or what disaster
can part me from his love?

We are not alone, Lord. You stand with us and you watch over us. Help us to stand with others in their time of need. Amen.

Wednesday, January 4 — Psalm 3
1 Chronicles 4:24–43; Acts 9:23–35

The angel of the Lord touched Elijah, and said, "Get up and eat, otherwise the journey will be too much for you." 1 Kings 19:7

Feed your lambs, I'll feed your lambs 601*
and first of all with food;
give them drink and comfort them
and build their fortitude;
then I'll feed them with the word
you fed me with until
they're ready, Lord, so ready, Lord,
to go and do your will.

Therefore, lift your drooping hands and strengthen your weak knees, and make straight paths for your feet. Hebrews 12:12-13

God, grant me strength to do 615
with ready heart and willing,
whatever you command,
my calling here fulfilling;
and do it when I ought,
with zeal and joyfulness;
and bless the work I've wrought,
for you must give success.

Merciful God, help us to remember that when we feel weak and are struggling, we can turn to you. Sustain us with your spirit and direct us through the day. In your name, we pray. Amen.

Thursday, January 5 — Psalm 4
1 Chronicles 5:1–22; Acts 9:36–10:8

O God, from my youth you have taught me, and I still proclaim your wondrous deeds. Psalm 71:17

I love to tell the story, 625
for those who know it best
seem hungering and thirsting
to hear it, like the rest.
And when, in scenes of glory,
I sing the new, new song,
I'll sing the old, old story
that I have loved so long.
I love to tell the story;
I'll sing this theme in glory
and tell the old, old story
of Jesus and his love.

Simeon said, "Lord, now you are letting your servant depart in peace, according to your word; for my eyes have seen your salvation which you have prepared before the face of all peoples." Luke 2:29-31 NKJV

Go now in peace, go now in peace; 822*
may the love of God surround you
ev'rywhere, ev'rywhere you may go.

Abiding God, you remain a constant source of comfort in our lives. We can see where your hand has been upon us in the past and we have hope for where you will lead us. We celebrate the promises fulfilled in our lives through your grace and love for us. Amen.

Epiphany

Watchword for the Epiphany — Arise, shine; for your light has come, and the glory of the Lord has risen upon you. Isaiah 60:1

Epiphany of the Lord — Isaiah 60:1-6; Psalm 72:1-7,10-14
Ephesians 3:1-12; Matthew 2:1-12

Friday, January 6 — Psalm 5
1 Chronicles 5:23–6:30; Acts 10:9–23a

Hezekiah became sick and was at the point of death. He prayed to the Lord, and he answered him and gave him a sign. But Hezekiah did not respond according to the benefit done to him for his heart was proud. 2 Chronicles 32:24-25

Come now, O Lord, and teach us how to pray. 742
Teach us to ask ourselves from day to day
if we are yours and yours alone will be
through earthly days and through eternity.

God opposes the proud, but gives grace to the humble. 1 Peter 5:5

Give deep humility; the sense 750
of godly sorrow give,
a strong desiring confidence
to hear your voice and live.

Give us humble hearts, gracious God, that we may see the world as you desire it to be and that we might know our place in it. In Jesus' name, we pray. Amen.

Saturday, January 7 — Psalm 6
1 Chronicles 6:31–81; Acts 10:23b–33

From the rising of the sun to its setting, the name of the Lord is to be praised. Psalm 113:3

To God all glory, praise, and love 548
be now and ever giv'n
by saints below and saints above,
the church in earth and heav'n.

May the God of steadfastness and encouragement grant you to live in harmony with one another, in accordance with Christ Jesus, so that together you may with one voice glorify the God and Father of our Lord Jesus Christ. Romans 15:5-6

You have led us by your Spirit 619*
to accept your kingdom's goal.
Hand in hand with joy advancing,
we are one in heart and soul,
filled by you with one great passion:
that the world may be made whole.

Lord, give us a spirit of cooperation and goodwill. Help us to see the pathway within our circumstance where we can journey alongside others for your glory. Amen.

First Sunday after Epiphany

Watchword for the week — A bruised reed he will not break, and a dimly burning wick he will not quench; he will faithfully bring forth justice. Isaiah 42:3

Sunday, January 8 — Isaiah 42:1-9; Psalm 29
Acts 10:34-43; Matthew 3:13-17

Give generously to your needy brother and do so without a grudging heart. Deuteronomy 15:10 NIV

In mercy, Lord, this grace bestow, 643
that in your service we may do
with gladness and a willing mind
whatever is for us assigned.

Give and it will be given to you. Luke 6:38

Teach us to love in truth, 801*
to give and to receive
with joyful and with open hearts,
with all that we believe;
to seek another's good,
to honor what is right,
to let our will and our desire
be held in holy light.

Lord, as you have been generous with us through the blessings of your limitless love, we pray that we may have that same generous spirit. Empower us to give freely to others in ways that would best serve them. Help us to give without judgement or fear, trusting in your providence for us all. In the name of Jesus, we pray. Amen.

Monday, January 9 — Psalm 7:1–9
1 Chronicles 7; Acts 10:34–43

You shall not join hands with the wicked to act as a malicious witness. Exodus 23:1

Help me walk in the paths of righteousness; 728*
be my aid when Satan and sin oppress.
I am trusting you whate'er may be.
Lead me, O Lord, lead me.

Finally, beloved, whatever is true, whatever is honorable, whatever is just, whatever is pure, whatever is pleasing, whatever is commendable, if there is any excellence and if there is anything worthy of praise, think about these things. Philippians 4:8

May the mind of Christ my Savior 585
live in me from day to day,
by his love and pow'r controlling
all I do and say.

Rock of ages, we pray for the strength to stand with unwavering conviction for faith, love, and hope. Keep our hearts grounded in your grace while we labor for your goodness in this world. Amen.

Tuesday, January 10 — Psalm 7:10–17
1 Chronicles 8; Acts 10:44–11:10

Moses said to God, "Who am I that I should go to Pharaoh, and bring the Israelites out of Egypt?" God said, "I will be with you." Exodus 3:11-12

My soul is waiting for the Lord 761*
as one who longs for morning;
no watcher waits with greater hope
than I for his returning.
I hope as Israel in the Lord;
he sends redemption through his word.
We praise him for his mercy.

Jesus said, "See, I am sending you out like sheep into the midst of wolves; so be wise as serpents and innocent as doves." Matthew 10:16

Forth in your name, O Lord, I go 638
my daily labor to pursue—
you only, Lord, resolved to know
in all I think or speak or do.

Lord, you are a God who sends. You sent your Son to us that we might be forgiven and restored to you. You now send us out as agents of your grace. We do not go by our own power or strength, but by trusting in you. Amen.

Wednesday, January 11 — Psalm 8
1 Chronicles 9:1–34; Acts 11:11–24

The Lord has heard my supplication, the Lord accepts my prayer. Psalm 6:9

Prayer is the burden of a sigh, 749
the falling of a tear,
the upward glancing of an eye,
when none but God is near.

Whenever you pray, go into your room and shut the door and pray to your Father who is in secret; and your Father who sees in secret will reward you. Matthew 6:6

God of grace and God of glory, 751*
on your people pour your power;
crown your ancient Church's story;
bring its bud to glorious flower.
Grant us wisdom, grant us courage
for the facing of this hour,
for the facing of this hour.

Lord, we thank you for your listening ear. In humility, we come to you with the burdens and concerns of our hearts, knowing that you care for us and we are not alone. We thank you for the assurance we find in this blessing. Amen.

* used by permission of Elinor Fosdick Downs.

Thursday, January 12 — Psalm 9:1–10
1 Chronicles 9:35–11:3; Acts 11:25–12:5

So now, O Israel, what does the Lord your God require of you? Only to fear the Lord your God, to walk in all his ways, to love him, to serve the Lord your God with all your heart and with all your soul. Deuteronomy 10:12

Help me to watch and pray 645
and on yourself rely,
assured, if I my trust betray,
I shall forever die.

Whoever obeys his word, truly in this person the love of God has reached perfection. 1 John 2:5

O Master, let me walk with you 735
in lowly paths of service true;
tell me your secret; help me bear
the strain of toil, the fret of care.

Divine Wisdom, help us to understand that obedience to your commandments leads us on the pathway of the liberating power of your love. We pray for the strength to surrender all and put our trust in you. Amen.

Friday, January 13 — Psalm 9:11–20
1 Chronicles 11:4–47; Acts 12:6–19

Do not fear, or be afraid; have I not told you from of old and declared it? You are my witnesses! Isaiah 44:8

We are called to be God's prophets, 635*
speaking for the truth and right,
standing firm for godly justice,
bringing evil things to light.
Let us seek the courage needed,
our high calling to fulfill,
that the world may know the blessing
of the doing of God's will.

So we are ambassadors for Christ, since God is making his appeal through us; we entreat you on behalf of Christ, be reconciled to God. 2 Corinthians 5:20

Christ for the world we sing! 640
The world to Christ we bring
with fervent prayer,
the wayward and the lost
by restless passions tossed,
redeemed at countless cost
from dark despair.

Holy Redeemer, as we face the needs of the world around us, help us to be bold in our witness, loving in our service, and overflowing with hope. It is for you that we bring the good news to the nations. Amen.

Saturday, January 14 — Psalm 10:1–11
1 Chronicles 12; Acts 12:20–13:7

Your eyes beheld my unformed substance. In your book were written all the days that were formed for me. Psalm 139:16

Know that the Lord is God indeed; 539
he formed us all without our aid.
We are the flock he comes to feed,
the sheep who by his hand were made.

Do not worry about your life. Matthew 6:25

Savior, like a shepherd lead us; 731
much we need your tender care;
in your pleasant pastures feed us,
for our use your folds prepare.
Blessed Jesus, blessed Jesus,
you have bought us; yours we are.
Blessed Jesus, blessed Jesus,
you have bought us; yours we are.

Savior, we lay our burdens down. Lord, we trust in your providence. Clear our minds and calm our hearts as we stand on your promises for now and for eternity. Amen.

Second Sunday after the Epiphany

Watchword for the Week — God is faithful; by him you were called into the fellowship of his Son, Jesus Christ our Lord. 1 Corinthians 1:9

Sunday, January 15 — Isaiah 49:1-7; Psalm 40:1-11
1 Corinthians 1:1-9; John 1:29-42

To do righteousness and justice is more acceptable to the Lord than sacrifice. Proverbs 21:3

What does the Lord require 695*
for praise and offering?
What sacrifice, desire, or tribute bid you bring?
Do justly, love mercy, walk humbly with your God.

For just as the body without the spirit is dead, so faith without works is also dead. James 2:26

My works of love and sacrifice, 776**
although required, cannot suffice.
His precious blood alone has been
sufficient ransom for my sin.

Loving God, raise us up to do the good you would have us do. Open our eyes, ears, and hearts to those who are oppressed and marginalized. May our efforts on their behalf glorify you. We pray this, in the name of Jesus. Amen.

Monday, January 16 — Psalm 10:12–18
1 Chronicles 13:1–14:7; Acts 13:8–20a

My lips will shout for joy when I sing praises to you; my soul also, which you have rescued. Psalm 71:23

Sing praise to God who reigns above, 537
the God of all creation,
the God of pow'r, the God of love,
the God of our salvation.
My soul with comfort rich he fills,
and ev'ry grief he gently stills:
to God all praise and glory!

Joyfully give thanks to the Father, who has enabled you to share in the inheritance of the saints in the light. Colossians 1:11-12

Joyful, joyful, we adore you, 544
God of glory, Lord of love;
hearts unfold like flow'rs before you,
op'ning to the sun above.
Melt the clouds of sin and sadness;
drive the dark of doubt away;
giver of immortal gladness,
fill us with the light of day!

God of constant delight, we thank you for your unlimited grace given to us. We stand with all those who have gone before us in a community of light that gives hope and healing. Amen.

Tuesday, January 17 — Psalm 11
1 Chronicles 14:8–15:29; Acts 13:20b–33

I treasure your word in my heart, so that I may not sin against you. Psalm 119:11

God's word alive and active, 503*
proclaimed throughout the years,
still comforts us when hurting
and calms our hidden fears.
God's word of truth and justice
sets weary captives free,
and joins God's holy people
in new community.

Guard the good treasure entrusted to you, with the help of the Holy Spirit living in us. 2 Timothy 1:14

Holy Spirit, still creating 496**
Christ's one church in tongues of flame,
move within us and inspire us
more to serve God's holy name.

Eternal Word, we are grateful that you have given us knowledge of your will for us through scripture and the Holy Spirit. We pray for the wisdom and strength to live out your will daily. Amen.

Wednesday, January 18 — Psalm 12
1 Chronicles 16:1–36; Acts 13:34–47

You in your mercy have led forth the people whom you have redeemed. Exodus 15:13 NKJV

Come, Almighty to deliver, 474
let us all your life receive;
suddenly return, and never,
never more your temple leave.
You we would be always blessing,
serve you as your hosts above,
pray, and praise you without ceasing,
glory in your perfect love.

Christ also suffered for sins once for all, the righteous for the unrighteous, in order to bring you to God. 1 Peter 3:18

When I survey the wondrous cross 350
on which the Prince of glory died,
my richest gain I count but loss,
and pour contempt on all my pride.

Living Redeemer, your sacrifice was for all, whether we chose to recognize you or not. Keep us among those who humbly remember and live in response to such unbelievable love. Amen.

Thursday, January 19 — Psalm 13
1 Chronicles 16:37–17:27; Acts 13:48–14:7

God looks to the ends of the earth, and sees everything under the heavens. Job 28:24

This is my Father's world, 456
and to my list'ning ears
all nature sings and round me rings
the music of the spheres.
This is my Father's world;
I rest me in the thought
of rocks and trees, of skies and seas—
his hand the wonders wrought.

It is not the will of your Father in heaven that one of these little ones should be lost. Matthew 18:14

O Christians, haste, your mission high fulfilling, 618
to tell to all the world that God is light,
that he who made all nations is not willing
one life should perish, lost in shades of night.

Lord, you watch over us, and that is no small thing. Help us to remember this when we are feeling alone and lost. Remind us to keep our eyes open for others who may also be feeling lost. Amen.

Friday, January 20 — Psalm 14
1 Chronicles 18; Acts 14:8–20

When you make a sale to your neighbor or buy from your neighbor, you shall not cheat one another. Leviticus 25:14

Let us each for others care, 672
each another's burden bear,
to your church a pattern give,
showing how believers live.

We intend to do what is right not only in the Lord's sight but also in the sight of others. 2 Corinthians 8:21

Dear Lord and Father of mankind, 739
forgive our foolish ways;
reclothe us in our rightful mind;
in purer lives thy service find,
in deeper rev'rence, praise.

God of justice, give us the wisdom and strength to act with honesty and integrity. Remind us of our responsibility to both you and our communities to hold ourselves to the highest standards of your grace. Amen.

Saturday, January 21 — Psalm 15
1 Chronicles 19,20; Acts 14:21–15:5

Naked I came from my mother's womb, and naked I will depart. Job 1:21 NIV

God has given, he has taken, 667*
but his children ne'er forsaken;
his the loving purpose solely
to preserve them pure and holy.

Clothe yourselves with the Lord Jesus Christ. Romans 13:14 NIV

Ten thousand times ten thousand 394
in sparkling raiment bright,
the armies of the ransomed saints
throng up the steeps of light!
'Tis finished, all is finished,
their fight with death and sin.
Fling open wide the golden gates
and let the victors in!

Lord, all the things in our lives will pass, but you will remain. Liberate us from the desire for things that really don't matter and increase our desire for you. Amen.

Third Sunday after Epiphany

Watchword for the week — The Lord is my light and my salvation; whom shall I fear? The Lord is the stronghold of my life; of whom shall I be afraid? Psalm 27:1

Sunday, January 22 — Isaiah 9:1-4; Psalm 27:1,4-9
1 Corinthians 1:10-18; Matthew 4:12-23

There is none like you, O Lord; you are great, and your name is great in might. Jeremiah 10:6

Mighty God, we humbly pray, 586
let your pow'r now lead the way
that in all things we may show
that we in your likeness grow.

No one can lay any foundation other than the one that has been laid; that foundation is Jesus Christ. 1 Corinthians 3:11

The church's one foundation 511
is Jesus Christ, her Lord;
she is his new creation
by water and the word;
from heav'n he came and sought her
to be his holy bride;
with his own blood he bought her,
and for her life he died.

Lord, keep us grounded in your love and aid us in the task of building opportunities for all to abide in your grace. Amen.

Monday, January 23 — Psalm 16:1–6
1 Chronicles 21:1–26; Acts 15:6–18

Do not let me be put to shame, for I take refuge in you. Psalm 25:20

You are my refuge; grant me, I pray, 796*
strength for each burden, light for each day,
comfort in sorrow, grace for tomorrow,
Savior divine!

The rain fell, the floods came, and the winds blew and beat on that house, but it did not fall, because it had been founded on rock. Matthew 7:25

If you but trust in God to guide you 712
and place your confidence in him,
you'll find him always there beside you
to give you hope and strength within;
for those who trust God's changeless love
build on the rock that will not move.

God, your love is our shield when the troubles of life would overwhelm us. The storms will pass as you remain our rock and our foundation. Thank you, Lord, for this comfort. Amen.

Tuesday, January 24 — Psalm 16:7–11
1 Chronicles 21:27–22:19; Acts 15:19–31

You have made the Most High your dwelling-place. Psalm 91:9

> What splendid rays of truth and grace, 596
> all other light excelling!
> This I know when he in love
> makes my heart his dwelling!

Jesus said, "Do not let your hearts be troubled. Believe in God, believe also in me." John 14:1

> Faith is a living power from heav'n 700
> that grasps the promise God has giv'n,
> a trust that can't be overthrown
> fixed heartily on Christ alone.

God of glory, we place our trust in you. Regardless of the challenges and circumstance of each day, help us stand on the promises of your love for us. In Jesus' name, we pray. Amen.

Wednesday, January 25 — Psalm 17:1–7
1 Chronicles 23; Acts 15:32–16:3

Whoever is steadfast in righteousness will live, but whoever pursues evil will die. Proverbs 11:19

I am thine, O Lord—I have heard thy voice, 607
and it told thy love to me;
but I long to rise in the arms of faith
and be closer drawn to thee.

Blessed are those who hunger and thirst for righteousness, for they will be filled. Matthew 5:6

You give yourself to us, O Lord; 417*
then selfless let us be
to serve each other in your name
in truth and charity.
You satisfy the hungry heart
with gift of finest wheat.
Come, give to us, O saving Lord,
the bread of life to eat.

Lord, we hunger for so many things when our greatest hunger should be for you. Give us the desire to labor for justice and righteousness in the face of the injustices we see all around us. Amen.

Thursday, January 26 — Psalm 17:8–15
1 Chronicles 24; Acts 16:4–15

You have put gladness in my heart more than when their grain and wine abound. Psalm 4:7

As grows the hidden seed 653*
to fruit that serves our need,
your kingdom grows.
So let our toil be used,
no gift of yours abused,
no humble task refused
your love bestows.

The kingdom of God is not food and drink but righteousness and peace and joy in the Holy Spirit. Romans 14:17

Holy Spirit, come, renew us, p226**
come yourself to make us live,
holy through your loving presence,
holy through the gifts you give.

God, fill our hearts with your Holy Spirit; sustain us with your power and strengthen our work for justice and peace in this world. Amen.

Friday, January 27 — Psalm 18:1–6
1 Chronicles 25; Acts 16:16–29

The righteous are like trees planted by streams of water, which yield their fruit in its season, and their leaves do not wither. Psalm 1:3

In the bulb there is a flower; 797*
in the seed, an apple tree;
in cocoons, a hidden promise:
butterflies will soon be free!
In the cold and snow of winter
there's a spring that waits to be,
unrevealed until its season,
something God alone can see.

Paul wrote: This is my prayer, that your love may abound more and more in knowledge and depth of insight, filled with the fruit of righteousness that comes through Jesus Christ—to the glory and praise of God. Philippians 1:9,11 NIV

Love divine, all loves excelling, 474
joy of heav'n, to earth come down!
Fix in us your humble dwelling,
all your faithful mercies crown.
Jesus, you are all compassion,
pure, unbounded love impart!
Visit us with your salvation,
enter ev'ry trembling heart.

Creator, we pray that the seeds of love you plant in us will grow, not just for our benefit, but so that we may serve others. May your love overflow from our lives and touch all who are in need. Amen.

Saturday, January 28 — Psalm 18:7–15
1 Chronicles 26; Acts 16:30–17:3

David said to the Philistine, "You come to me with sword and spear and javelin; but I come to you in the name of the Lord of hosts." 1 Samuel 17:45

We've a song to be sung to the nations, 621
that shall lift their hearts to the Lord,
a song that shall conquer evil
and shatter the spear and sword,
and shatter the spear and sword.

Do not conform to the pattern of this world. Romans 12:2 NIV

Jesus calls us from the worship 600
of the vain world's golden store,
from each idol that would keep us,
saying, "Christian, love me more."

Source of justice, strengthen us to face the challenges of this day empowered by your transforming love. We ask for boldness to speak and act in hope against the violence, fear, and anxiety that harms us all. In Jesus' name, we pray. Amen.

Fourth Sunday after Epiphany

Watchword for the week — For the message about the cross is foolishness to those who are perishing, but to us who are being saved it is the power of God. 1 Corinthians 1:18

Sunday, January 29 — Micah 6:1-8; Psalm 15
1 Corinthians 1:18-31; Matthew 5:1-12

Restore us, O Lord God of hosts; let your face shine, that we may be saved. Psalm 80:19

Lord of all life, below, above, 464
whose light is truth, whose warmth is love,
before your ever-blazing throne
we ask no luster of our own.

By the tender mercy of our God, the dawn from on high will break upon us, to give light to those who sit in darkness. Luke 1:78-79

People in darkness are looking for light, 266*
come, come, come Jesus Christ;
people with blindness are longing for sight,
come, Lord Jesus Christ.
These days of adventure when all people wait
are days for the advent of Love.

Light of the world, empower us to carry your light to all. Make us beacons of love and encouragement, filled with patience and humility as we serve the world around us. In Jesus' name, we pray. Amen.

Monday, January 30 — Psalm 18:16–24
1 Chronicles 27; Acts 17:4–15

The Lord our God protected us along all the way that we went. Joshua 24:17

He leadeth me: O blessed thought! 787
O words with heav'nly comfort fraught!
Whate'er I do, where'er I be,
still 'tis God's hand that leadeth me.

And remember, I am with you always, to the end of the age. Matthew 28:20

Great is thy faithfulness, O God my Father, 460*
there is no shadow of turning with thee;
thou changest not, thy compassions they fail not;
as thou hast been thou forever wilt be.

God of all comfort, no matter what our circumstances may be, you remain faithful to us. Thank you for your abiding presence throughout our journey of life and faith. Amen.

Tuesday, January 31 — Psalm 18:25–29
1 Chronicles 28,29; Acts 17:16–28

God, you remain the same, and your years will never end. Psalm 102:27 NIV

Let not the passing of the years 804*
rob us of joy or cause us fears;
and make our faith, O Lord, hold true,
that we may always rest in you.

Grace to you and peace from him who is and who was and who is to come. Revelation 1:4

As it was without beginning, 458
so it lasts without an end;
to their children's children ever
shall God's righteousness extend.

Rock of ages, we are so grateful because, in the storms of our lives and the tumult of our times, you remain the same. It is on you we stand secure and know peace. In Jesus' name, we pray. Amen.

Wednesday, February 1 — Psalm 18:30–36
2 Chronicles 1,2; Acts 17:29–18:7

Return to me, says the Lord of hosts, and I will return to you. Zechariah 1:3

With grateful joy and holy fear, 785*
God's charity we learn;
let us with heart and mind and soul
now love God in return.

The Lord is patient with you, not wanting any to perish, but all to come to repentance. 2 Peter 3:9

When we seek relief 799
from a long-felt grief,
when temptations come alluring,
make us patient and enduring;
show us that bright shore
where we weep no more.

O Gracious King, our sins are many and we sometimes stray, yet your patience with us knows no bounds. As you call us to return, may we come to you with repentance and the hope for everlasting life. In your name, we pray. Amen.

Thursday, February 2 — Psalm 18:37–45
2 Chronicles 3:1–5:1; Acts 18:8–21

I am watching over my word to perform it. Jeremiah 1:12

O give me Samuel's ear! 609
The open ear, O Lord,
alive and quick to hear
each whisper of thy word;
like him to answer at thy call,
and to obey thee first of all.

Jesus said, "Do not think that I have come to abolish the law or the prophets; I have come not to abolish but to fulfill." Matthew 5:17

One our Master, one alone, 525
none but Christ as Lord we own;
*"brethren of his law" are we—
"As I loved you, so love ye."
Branches we in Christ, the Vine,
living by his life divine;
as the Father with the Son,
so, in Christ, we all are one.

Loving Master, over the millennia your sons and daughters told us of your power and love. You gave us laws to live by and the words of your prophets told of glories to come. We rejoice that those words have been fulfilled in the sacrifice of your Son. In His name, we give you thanks. Amen.

* This was a name applied to itself by the Moravian Church in the fifteenth century.

Friday, February 3 — Psalm 18:46–50
2 Chronicles 5:2–6:23; Acts 18:22–19:5

You turn things upside down! Shall the potter be regarded as the clay? Shall the thing made say of its maker, "He did not make me"; or the thing formed say of the one who formed it, "He has no understanding?" Isaiah 29:16

His sov'reign pow'r without our aid 455
formed us of clay and gave us breath;
and when like wand'ring sheep we strayed,
he saved us from the pow'r of death.

We are what he has made us, created in Christ Jesus for good works. Ephesians 2:10

Soar we now where Christ has led, alleluia! 359
Foll'wing our exalted Head; alleluia!
Made like him, like him we rise; alleluia!
Ours the cross, the grave, the skies. Alleluia!

Heavenly Potter, we know you brought us into the world to do your will, yet there are times when we question the source of our being. Help us to understand that you alone are the true power behind our lives, and that those lives are to be lived in your service. In your name, we pray. Amen.

Saturday, February 4 — Psalm 19:1–6
2 Chronicles 6:24–7:22; Acts 19:6–20

Jacob made a vow, saying to God, "Of all that you give me I will surely give one-tenth to you." Genesis 28:20,22

We give you but your own 657
in any gifts we bring;
all that we have is yours alone,
a trust from you, our King.

The one who sows sparingly will also reap sparingly, and the one who sows bountifully will also reap bountifully. 2 Corinthians 9:6

Father, we praise you; 535*
Jesus, we love you;
Spirit, we thank you,
for these new days;
help us to know, Lord;
help us to grow, Lord;
help us to sow, Lord,
your love always.

Faithful Gardener, you bestow upon us the unimaginable bounty of your love. All that we are, we owe to you. May we, in turn, give generously of ourselves to bring about your kingdom. Help us to grow, Lord, and help us to sow your love always. Amen.

Fifth Sunday after Epiphany

Watchword for the week — For I decided to know nothing among you except Jesus Christ, and him crucified. 1 Corinthians 2:2

Sunday, February 5 — Isaiah 58:1-9a,(9b-12); Psalm 112:1-9,(10) 1 Corinthians 2:1-12,(13-16); Matthew 5:13-20

When times are good, be happy; but when times are bad, consider this: God has made the one as well as the other. Therefore, no one can discover anything about their future. Ecclesiastes 7:14 NIV

Be still, my soul: your God will undertake 757
to guide the future, as in ages past.
Your hope, your confidence, let nothing shake;
all now mysterious shall be bright at last.
Be still, my soul: the waves and winds still know
the Christ who ruled them while he dwelt below.

Look at the birds of the air; they neither sow nor reap nor gather into barns, and yet your heavenly Father feeds them. Are you not of more value than they? Matthew 6:26

God gave us eyes to see them, 467
and lips that we might tell
how great is God Almighty,
who has made all things well.

Divine Creator, you make and care for all we know, yet much about you is unknowable. Give us strength during those times when we fail to understand your mystery, and help us know that no matter what, you feed us with your love. In your name, we pray. Amen.

Monday, February 6 — Psalm 19:7–14
2 Chronicles 8:1–9:12; Acts 19:21–31

The heart is devious above all else; it is perverse—who can understand it? I the Lord test the mind and search the heart, to give to all according to their ways. Jeremiah 17:9-10

Praise the source of faith and learning 664*
who has sparked and stoked the mind
with a passion for discerning
how the world has been designed.
Let the sense of wonder flowing
from the wonders we survey
keep our faith forever growing
and renew our need to pray.

So let us not grow weary in doing what is right, for we will reap at harvest time, if we do not give up. Galatians 6:9

To hail your rising, Sun of life, 320
the gath'ring nations come
with joy, as when the reapers bear
their harvest treasures home.

Holy Teacher, you test our minds and search our hearts for the good we can offer the world. Help us grow that good, never surrender to evil or sloth, and endeavor to love you with all of our hearts, our souls, and our minds. Amen.

Tuesday, February 7 — Psalm 20
2 Chronicles 9:13–10:19; Acts 19:32–20:3

As the rain and the snow come down from heaven, and do not return there until they have watered the earth, making it bring forth and sprout, giving seed to the sower and bread to the eater, so shall my word be that goes out from my mouth. Isaiah 55:10-11

> Living water, never ending, 767*
> quench the thirst and flood the soul.
> Wellspring, source of life eternal,
> drench our dryness, make us whole.

If you abide in me, and my words abide in you, ask for whatever you wish, and it will be done for you. My Father is glorified by this, that you bear much fruit and become my disciples. John 15:7-8

> Hear us, O Lord, as we now pray, 536**
> dedicate us to your way;
> lead us to work that bears your fruit,
> giving knowledge of your truth.
> Open our door and enter in,
> rescue from darkness and from sin.
> Strengthen according to your might,
> share with us the promised life.

Generous Provider, you give us all we need to grow in faith, love, and hope. We are sustained by your heavenly waters and the love of your Son, who rescues us from darkness and sin. May our words and deeds bear fruit by bringing those in need to you. In Jesus' name, we pray. Amen.

Wednesday, February 8 — Psalm 21
2 Chronicles 11:1–12:12; Acts 20:4–16

Our heart is glad in the Lord, because we trust in his holy name. Psalm 33:21

This is my Father's world: 456
he shines in all that's fair;
in rustling grass I hear him pass—
he speaks to me ev'rywhere.
This is my Father's world:
why should my heart be sad?
The Lord is King, let heaven ring!
God reigns; let earth be glad.

Rejoice always, pray without ceasing.
1 Thessalonians 5:16-17

God with us, God with us, 324
God made known in human frame;
in his name rejoice with gladness,
since to save the lost he came;
none need sink in hopeless sadness,
for Immanuel is now with us,
God with us, God with us.

Rejoice, believers, rejoice! Lord, we know you as our trusting, loving, generous God, who gave us his Son so that we may be saved from hopeless sadness. We know, too, that you are with us always. May we rejoice in your holy name, for it gladdens our hearts. Amen.

Thursday, February 9 — Psalm 22:1–8
2 Chronicles 12:13–13:22; Acts 20:17–31

Be silent before the Lord God! For the day of the Lord is at hand. Zephaniah 1:7

Lead on, O King eternal! 753
The day of march has come;
henceforth in fields of conquest
your tents will be our home:
through days of preparation
your grace has made us strong,
and now, O King eternal,
we lift our battle song.

Therefore you also must be ready, for the Son of Man is coming at an unexpected hour. Matthew 24:44

Eat and rest at this great feast, p206
then to serve him freely go,
at it is for pilgrims fit,
as disciples ought to do.
We, when Jesus we shall see
coming in his majesty,
shall the marriage supper share,
if we his true followers are.

Holy Redeemer, we await the hour of your return with hope and anticipation. While all we do should prepare us for that day, may we also live lives that demonstrate to all that your kingdom is at hand today. With hope, we pray. Amen.

Friday, February 10 — Psalm 22:9–21
2 Chronicles 14,15; Acts 20:32–21:4

How beautiful on the mountains are the feet of those who bring good news, who proclaim peace, who bring good tidings, who proclaim salvation, who say to Zion, "Your God reigns!" Isaiah 52:7 NIV

Now let all the heav'ns adore you, 258
let saints and angels sing before you
with harp and cymbal's clearest tone.
Of one pearl each shining portal,
where, joining with the choir immortal,
we gather round your radiant throne.
No eye has seen that light,
no ear the echoed might
of your glory;
yet there shall we in your vict'ry
sing shouts of praise eternally!

As shoes for your feet put on whatever will make you ready to proclaim the gospel of peace. Ephesians 6:15

"Comfort, comfort now my people; 264
tell of peace!" So says our God.
Comfort those who sit in darkness
bowed beneath oppression's load.
To God's people now proclaim
that God's pardon waits for them!
Tell them that their war is over;
God will reign in peace forever!

Bringer of peace, our world struggles to live in harmony. Our leaders choose war over compromise, battle over benevolence, and anger over forgiveness. Yet, if they only heard your word and walked your way, ours would be a world in unison. We pray for peace. Amen.

Saturday, February 11 — Psalm 22:22–28
2 Chronicles 16,17; Acts 21:5–16

Bring me out of prison, so that I may give thanks to your name. Psalm 142:7

Long my imprisoned spirit lay 773
fast bound in sin and nature's night.
Your sunrise turned that night to day;
I woke—the dungeon flamed with light!
My chains fell off, your voice I knew;
was freed, I rose, and followed you.
My chains fell off, your voice I knew;
was freed, I rose, and followed you.

So if the Son makes you free, you will be free indeed. John 8:36

Come, O long-expected Jesus, 262
born to set your people free;
from our fears and sins release us;
O, in you our rest shall be.
Israel's strength and consolation,
hope to all the earth impart,
dear desire of ev'ry nation,
joy of ev'ry longing heart.

Loving Sustainer, many of us find ourselves prisoners of our thoughts, deeds, and longings. We thank you for giving us your son, born to break the chains that keep us from you. Help us to overcome fear and oppression and help us share your message of freedom and peace. Amen.

Sixth Sunday after Epiphany

Watchword for the week — Choose life so that you and your descendants may live, loving the Lord your God, obeying him, and holding fast to him. Deuteronomy 30:19,20

Sunday, February 12 — Deuteronomy 30:15-20; Psalm 119:1-8
1 Corinthians 3:1-9; Matthew 5:21-37

Take good care to love the Lord your God, to walk in all his ways. Joshua 22:5

O let us know you always near, p204
as is the light that shines so clear,
or as the air we breathe;
in all our thoughts, our words and ways,
thus may our lives show forth your praise,
our hearts be freed from things beneath.

Whoever serves me must follow me, and where I am, there will my servant be also. John 12:26

Chosen flock, your faithful Shepherd follow, 444
who laid down his life for you;
all your days unto his service hallow,
each to be disciples true;
evermore rejoice to do his pleasure,
be the fullness of his grace your treasure;
should success your labor crown,
give the praise to him alone.

Abiding Shepherd, your nearness is our joy and guide. By your presence, we receive light for our path and purpose for our lives. May our lives demonstrate our gratitude for your love and ministry to us. We long to praise you, not only with our voices, but with lives of service to your children. Amen.

Monday, February 13 — Psalm 22:29–31
2 Chronicles 18; Acts 21:17–30

Do not cast me away from your presence, and do not take your holy spirit from me. Psalm 51:11

Create in me a clean heart, O God, p79
and renew a right spirit within me.
Cast me not away from your presence,
and take not your Holy Spirit from me.
Restore unto me the joy of salvation;
anoint me with your Spirit free.
Create in me a clean heart, O God,
and renew a right spirit within me.

The tax collector, standing far off, would not even look up to heaven, but was beating his breast and saying, "God, be merciful to me, a sinner!" Luke 18:13

Savior, now with contrite hearts 741
we approach your throne of love,
asking pardon for our sins,
peace and comfort from above.
You once suffered on the cross
to atone for sinners' guilt;
may we never, Lord, forget
that for us your blood was spilled.

Merciful God, we recognize that we are the objects of your love, not by our own doing, but by your unmerited grace. Renew us by your Spirit and hold us in your loving embrace. Draw us ever nearer to yourself that our lives might overflow with joy and gratitude for your tender mercies. Amen.

Tuesday, February 14 — Psalm 23
2 Chronicles 19:1–20:19; Acts 21:31–22:2

Surely God is good to Israel, to those who are pure in heart. Psalm 73: 1 NIV

Lord, we your presence seek; 584
we ask this blessing true:
give us a pure and lowly heart,
a temple fit for you.

Blessed are the pure in heart, for they will see God. Matthew 5:8

Breathe on me, breath of God, 494
until my heart is pure,
until with you I will one will
to do or to endure.

O God of Israel, for your temples, you have chosen neither stone nor wood. You chose our very hearts to be your dwelling place. By your spirit, may we keep our hearts pure and true—a fitting home for you. Amen.

Wednesday, February 15 — Psalm 24
2 Chronicles 20:20–21:17; Acts 22:3–16

I will again do amazing things with this people, shocking and amazing. The wisdom of their wise shall perish, and the discernment of the discerning shall be hidden. Isaiah 29:14

> Be thou my wisdom, and thou my true word; 719
> I ever with thee and thou with me, Lord;
> thou my great Father, I thy true son;
> thou in me dwelling, and I with thee one.

The crowd was amazed when they saw the mute speaking, the maimed whole, the lame walking, and the blind seeing. And they praised the God of Israel. Matthew 15:31

> Praise to the Lord, the almighty, 530
> the King of creation!
> O my soul, praise him,
> for he is your health and salvation!
> Let all who hear
> now to his temple draw near,
> joining in glad adoration.

Source of wisdom and wonder, your way and wisdom are higher and truer than anything we could devise. The works of your creative hands and your transforming touch overwhelm us with wonder and adoration. May your living word be our only wisdom, and the works of your hands be our constant inspiration. Amen.

Thursday, February 16 — Psalm 25:1–7
2 Chronicles 21:18–23:21; Acts 22:17–29

I called to the Lord out of my distress, and he answered me. Jonah 2:2

We come to you, our Father, 433
with thoughts of thanks and praise,
for your abundant mercy,
and all your love and grace;
we praise you for your goodness
and for your loving care,
for daily show'rs of blessing,
for answers to our prayers.

Jesus said, "Even the hairs of your head are all counted. Do not be afraid!" Luke 12:7

"Fear not, I am with you; O be not dismayed, 709
for I am your God and will still give you aid;
I'll strengthen you, help you and cause you to stand
upheld by my righteous, omnipotent hand."

Merciful Deliverer, in all the challenges of our lives, you are sufficient. In our times of need, may we turn to you in confidence, trusting in your presence with us and love for us. May we live by your strength and the assurance that nothing can part us from your eternal love nor keep us from our eternal home. Amen.

Friday, February 17 — Psalm 25:8–22
2 Chronicles 24:1–25:4; Acts 22:30–23:11

O Lord, how manifold are your works! In wisdom you have made them all; the earth is full of your creatures. Psalm 104:24

For the beauty of each hour 538
of the day and of the night,
hill and vale, and tree and flow'r,
sun and moon, and stars of light,
Lord of all, to you we raise
this our hymn of grateful praise.

You are worthy, our Lord and God, to receive glory and honor and power, for you created all things, and by your will they existed and were created. Revelation 4:11

O Lord my God, when I in awesome wonder 465*
consider all the works thy hands have made,
I see the stars, I hear the mighty thunder,
thy pow'r throughout the universe displayed.
Then sings my soul, my Savior God, to thee;
how great thou art, how great thou art!
Then sings my soul, my Savior God, to thee:
how great thou art, how great thou art!

Holy and almighty Creator, if we were only to open our eyes in faith, we would see your undeniable fingerprints on the galaxies in the heavens, the wonders of the earth, and the abundant forms of life in our world. Help us open our eyes to see how great you are! Amen.

Saturday, February 18 — Psalm 26
2 Chronicles 25:5–26:15; Acts 23:12–24

Whom have I in heaven but you? And there is nothing on earth that I desire other than you. Psalm 73:25

When the Lord appears, 594
this my spirit cheers;
when, his love to me revealing
he, the Sun of grace, with healing
in his beams appears,
this my spirit cheers.

I am convinced that neither death, nor life, nor angels, nor rulers, nor things present, nor things to come, nor powers, nor height, nor depth, nor anything else in all creation, will be able to separate us from the love of God in Christ Jesus our Lord. Romans 8:38-39

For the love of God is broader 185r
than the measure of man's mind;
and the heart of the eternal
is most wonderfully kind.

Divine Companion, your presence in our lives may not eliminate the tough times, but no difficulty can separate us from you. You are always with us, even in the darkest of times. Even when all else may be gone, you remain. May we always turn to you for comfort, peace, and hope. Amen.

Last Sunday after Epiphany

Watchword for the week — God said, "This is my Son, the Beloved; with him I am well pleased; listen to him!" Matthew 17:5

Sunday, February 19 — Exodus 24:12-18; Psalm 2
2 Peter 1:16-21; Matthew 17:1-9

By day the Lord commands his steadfast love, and at night his song is with me, a prayer to the God of my life. Psalm 42:8

Lord, may I be at rest in you 569
and sweetly sleep the whole night through.
Refresh my strength for your own sake,
so I may serve you when I wake.

And after Jesus had dismissed the crowds, he went up the mountain by himself to pray. When evening came, he was there alone. Matthew 14:23

O Sabbath rest by Galilee! 739
O calm of hills above,
where Jesus knelt to share with thee
the silence of eternity,
interpreted by love!

O Holy One, there is nowhere that we might go where you are not already there. May we remember that you are always with us and only a prayer away. May we remember to seek you in times of silence, free from distractions, and better able to discern your presence and commune with you. Amen.

Monday, February 20 — Psalm 27:1–6
2 Chronicles 26:16–28:8; Acts 23:25–24:3

"A mortal, born of woman, few of days and full of trouble, comes up like a flower and withers, flees like a shadow and does not last." Job 14:1-2

Lifegiving Creator of both great and small; 457
of all life the maker, the true life of all;
we blossom, then wither like leaves on the tree,
but you live forever who was and will be.

Here we have no lasting city, but we are looking for the city that is to come. Hebrews 13:14

How lovely is that city, 814
the home of God's elect!
How beautiful the country
that eager hearts expect!
O Christ, in mercy bring us
to that eternal shore
where Father, Son, and Spirit
are worshiped evermore.

Eternal Creator, although our days in this life are numbered, we take comfort in the assurance that, just as you have neither beginning nor ending, so your love for us never ends. May your eternal love for us empower us to look to the future with holy expectation and confidence. Amen.

Tuesday, February 21 — Psalm 27:7–14
2 Chronicles 28:9–29:19; Acts 24:4–16

David said to the Lord, "I have sinned greatly in what I have done. But now, O Lord, I pray you, take away the guilt of your servant." 2 Samuel 24:10

Now we bring ourselves to you; 741
cleanse us, Lord, we humbly pray;
undeserving though we be,
draw us closer ev'ry day.
Lord, our refuge, hope, and strength!
Keep, O keep us safe from harm,
shield us through our earthly life
by your everlasting arm.

If we confess our sins, he who is faithful and just will forgive us our sins and cleanse us from all unrighteousness. 1 John 1:9

Just as I am, and waiting not 762
to rid my soul of one dark blot,
to thee, whose blood can cleanse each spot,
O Lamb of God, I come, I come!

O Lamb of God, we are an imperfect people. All have sinned and fallen short of your will. Forgive us when we have strayed: for the evil we have done and good we have left undone. Cleanse us of our sin and renew us by your love. Amen.

Ash Wednesday — Joel 2:1-2,12-17; Psalm 51:1-17
2 Corinthians 5:20b-6:10; Matthew 6:1-6,16-21

Wednesday, February 22 — Psalm 28
2 Chronicles 29:20–30:27; Acts 24:17–27

Sing to the Lord; praise the Lord! For he has delivered the life of the needy from the hands of evildoers. Jeremiah 20:13

Open now the crystal fountain 790
where the healing waters flow;
let the fire and cloudy pillar
lead me all my journey through.
Strong deliv'rer, strong deliv'rer,
ever be my strength and shield;
ever be my strength and shield.

Mary said, "My soul magnifies the Lord, and my spirit rejoices in God my Savior, for he has looked with favor on the lowliness of his servant." Luke 1:46-48

We too should be voicing 448*
our love and rejoicing;
with glad adoration a song let us raise,
till all things now living
unite in thanksgiving:
to God in the highest,
hosanna and praise!

Strong Deliverer, we begin our Lenten journey with you today. Open our hearts and our minds anew to your sacrifice for us in order that we might know that God's love for us is limitless, with neither beginning nor end. Amen.

Thursday, February 23 — Psalm 29
2 Chronicles 31; Acts 25:1–15

Turn back from your evil ways; for why will you die? Ezekiel 33:11

Seek the Lord, whose willing presence 780*
moves your heart to make appeal.
Turn from wickedness and evil;
God will pardon, cleanse, and heal.

Rescue us from the evil one. Matthew 6:13

Though Satan should buffet, 754
though trials should come,
let this blessed assurance control,
that Christ has regarded my helpless estate,
and has shed his own blood for my soul.
It is well with my soul,
it is well, it is well with my soul.

O gracious Savior, we thank you that, in your divine mercy and grace, you have done for us what we were unable or unwilling to do for ourselves. You have called us to yourself. You have forgiven our sins, cleansed our hearts and lives, and healed us of our brokenness. Because of you, in all circumstances, we are able to sing, "It is well with my soul." Amen.

Friday, February 24 — Psalm 30:1–5
2 Chronicles 32; Acts 25:16–26:1

I will make with you an everlasting covenant. Isaiah 55:3

As it was without beginning, 458
so it lasts without an end;
to their children's children ever
shall God's righteousness extend:
unto such as keep God's cov'nant
and are steadfast in his way,
unto those who still remember
the commandments and obey.

In Christ every one of God's promises is a "Yes." For this reason it is through him that we say the "Amen," to the glory of God. 2 Corinthians 1:20

Praise to the Lord! 530
O, let all that is in me adore him!
All that has life and breath,
come now with praises before him!
Let the amen
sound from his people again.
Gladly forever adore him!

Great Promise-keeper, in Jesus Christ, all of your promises and all of our hopes were fulfilled. We are loved. We are forgiven. We are saved. May our lives continue to sound forth the praise of which you are worthy. Gladly, forever, may we adore you. Amen.

Saturday, February 25 — Psalm 30:6–12
2 Chronicles 33:1–34:7; Acts 26:2–14

Hear the word of the Lord, because the Lord has a charge to bring against you who live in the land: "There is no faithfulness, no love, no acknowledgment of God in the land." Hosea 4:1 NIV

For the Lord our God shall come 450
and shall take his harvest-home,
he himself in that great day
all offense shall take away,
give his angels charge at last
in the fire the weeds to cast,
but the fruitful ears to store
in his garner evermore.

If any of you is lacking in wisdom, ask God, who gives to all generously and ungrudgingly, and it will be given you. James 1:5

Be with me, Lord, where'er I go; 733
teach me what you would have me do;
suggest whate'er I think or say;
direct me in the narrow way.

Great Father, how often have you looked at the fields of our lives and found no harvest. Forgive us for the fruit we have failed to bear and the weeds we have sown. We thank you that you look to us not as a judge, but as a guide. Thank you for your wisdom, for showing us the better way. Thank you for the home you have prepared, even for sinners such as us. Amen.

First Sunday in Lent

Watchword for the week — Be glad in the Lord and rejoice, O righteous, and shout for joy, all you upright in heart. Psalm 32:11

Sunday, February 26 — Genesis 2:15-17;3:1-7; Psalm 32
Romans 5:12-19; Matthew 4:1-11

The Lord will keep your foot from being caught. Proverbs 3:26

Strike from our feet the fetters that bind. 489
Lift from our lives the weight of our wrong.
Teach us to love with heart, soul, and mind.
Spirit of God, your love makes us strong.

Jesus prayed, "I am not asking you to take them out of the world, but I ask you to protect them from the evil one." John 17:15

When I tread the verge of Jordan, 790
bid my anxious fears subside;
death of death and hell's destruction,
land me safe on Canaan's side.
Songs and praises, songs and praises,
I will sing forevermore;
I will sing forevermore.

Divine Protector, we thank you that you do not stand far off, keeping score of our faults. You observe us as a loving parent, anxious to prevent us from going astray and assisting us in learning the better way. Your desire is to deliver us from evil and place our feet upon the better path. Heavenly Father, we praise you for your nurturing love. Amen.

Monday, February 27 — Psalm 31:1–5
2 Chronicles 34:8–33; Acts 26:15–27

The Lord is coming to judge the earth. He will judge the world with righteousness, and the peoples with equity. Psalm 98:9

Hail to the Lord's anointed! 263
Great David's greater Son!
Hail, in the time appointed,
his reign on earth begun!
He comes to break oppression,
to set the captive free,
to take away transgression,
and rule in equity.

Lord, who will not fear and glorify your name? For you alone are holy. All nations will come and worship before you, for your judgments have been revealed. Revelation 15:4

Before the Lord's eternal throne, 455
you nations, bow with sacred joy;
know that the Lord is God alone;
he can create, and he destroy.

O righteous Judge, as you weigh the nations and people of the world in the scale of your will, we are comforted that you are motivated by love for all your children with an eye toward justice and equity. May we look to your reign as an expression of your love and as a longing for the fulfillment of justice for all your children. Amen.

Tuesday, February 28 — Psalm 31:6–9
2 Chronicles 35; Acts 26:28–27:8

Out of the depths I cry to you, O Lord. Lord, hear my voice! Psalm 130:1-2

Out of the depths I cry to you; 761*
O Father, hear me calling.
Incline your ear to my distress
in spite of my rebelling.
Do not regard my sinful deeds.
Send me the grace my spirit needs;
without it I am nothing.

The blind man shouted, "Jesus, Son of David, have mercy on me!" Those who were in front sternly ordered him to be quiet; but he shouted even more loudly, "Son of David, have mercy on me!" Luke 18:38-39

O Lamb of God, Lord Jesus Christ, 472**
whom God the Father gave us,
who for the world was sacrificed
upon the cross to save us,
at God's right hand you intercede
for those who for your mercy plead;
receive the prayer we offer.

O merciful Savior, too often our prayers are limited to times when we are in distress and call on you for help. May your Holy Spirit move within our hearts to call us to prayers of praise and gratitude for your goodness and blessing of our lives. Amen.

March 1, 1457:
Beginning of the Unity of the Brethren in Bohemia

Wednesday, March 1 — Psalm 31:10–20
2 Chronicles 36; Acts 27:9–20

The king said to Daniel, "Truly, your God is God of gods and Lord of kings." Daniel 2:47

Triumphant hosts on high 468
give thanks to God and sing,
and "Holy, holy, holy," cry,
"Almighty King!"
Hail, Abraham's God and ours!
One mighty hymn we raise.
All pow'r and majesty be yours
and endless praise!

Paul said, "King Agrippa, do you believe the prophets? I know that you do believe." Then Agrippa said to Paul, "You almost persuade me to become a Christian." Acts 26:27-28 NKJV

Let all who have received Christ 434*
now live life in the Lord
abounding in thanksgiving
for God's affirming word.
To us are given glad hearts
as we reflect Love's grace.
We know who we are called to be.
Now claiming our identity
as God's own people let us be
a living alleluia!

Lord, some days our faith is strong—some days we are only "almost persuaded." Lord God, work to persuade us and those holding power in human affairs, that our true identity is found as creatures who are loved by you and who, in response, are serving you. Amen.

Thursday, March 2 — Psalm 31:21–24
Ezra 1,2; Acts 27:21–38

The Lord said to Jacob, "Know that I am with you and will keep you wherever you go, and will bring you back to this land." Genesis 28:15

Great is thy faithfulness, O God my Father, 460*
there is no shadow of turning with thee;
thou changest not, thy compassions they fail not;
as thou hast been thou forever wilt be.

The one who calls you is faithful, and he will do this. 1 Thessalonians 5:24

Great is thy faithfulness! 460*
Great is thy faithfulness!
Morning by morning new mercies I see;
all I have needed thy hand hath provided;
great is thy faithfulness, Lord, unto me!

Faithful One, our world is filled with unfaithfulness—in our families, in our neighborhoods, in our government, in our businesses. Help us remain faithful wherever we go. In Jesus' name, we pray. Amen.

Friday, March 3 — Psalm 32
Ezra 3; Acts 27:39–28:6

You have set my feet in a broad place. Psalm 31:8

Commit thou all that grieves thee 177r
into the faithful hands
of him who never leaves thee,
who heaven and earth commands;
for he, the clouds' director,
whom winds and seas obey,
will be thy kind protector
and will prepare thy way.

I pray that the eyes of your heart may be enlightened in order that you may know the hope to which he has called you. Ephesians 1:18 NIV

My soul, then, with assurance 177r
hope still, be not dismayed;
he will from each encumbrance
again lift up thy head;
beyond thy wish extended
his goodness will appear,
when he hath fully ended
what caused thy needless fear.

Lord of history, the psalmist and our ancestors believed all things are in your control. Perhaps we have a clearer sense of both our human powers and our human limits. Increase our confidence, that in the end, you will heal and restore your creation. Amen.

Saturday, March 4 — Psalm 33:1–5
Ezra 4; Acts 28:7–16

The promises of the Lord are promises that are pure, silver refined in a furnace on the ground, purified seven times. Psalm 12:6

Spirit of God, burst forth in flame, 491*
searing our conscience, staking your claim.
Burn up the clutter, brand us apart;
warm ev'ry recess of my cold heart.

The words that I have spoken to you are spirit and life. John 6:63

Fill us with Spirit, fill us with joy! 491*
Your life to inherit, your gifts to employ;
your love to embody, great God within,
Spirit of Christ, let that new life begin!

Living Fire, from you comes our life, new each day. Refine us to be better tools for your work. Burn away what stands in the way of your work. Bring the warmth of new life. Open us to your work within us and among us. Amen.

Second Sunday in Lent

Watchword for the week — For God so loved the world that he gave his only Son, so that everyone who believes in him may not perish but may have eternal life. John 3:16

Sunday, March 5 — Genesis 12:1-4a; Psalm 121
Romans 4:1-5,13-17; John 3:1-17

The Lord spoke and it came to be; he commanded, and it stood firm. Psalm 33:9

Wide as the world is your command, 455
vast as eternity your love;
firm as a rock your truth must stand,
when rolling years shall cease to move.

The centurion answered, "Lord, I am not worthy to have you come under my roof; but only speak the word, and my servant will be healed." Matthew 8:8

My heart is weak and poor 604
until it master find;
it has no spring of action sure,
it varies with the wind.*
It cannot freely move
till you have wrought its chain;
enslave it with your matchless love,
and deathless it shall reign.

"Make me a captive, Lord, and then I shall be free." What a seeming contradiction! What a promise! We are at our best, not when we are alone, but when we are connected both to you and to one another. Lord, capture us. Amen.

* wind, as in a spring-driven music box.

Monday, March 6 — Psalm 33:6–11
Ezra 5:1–6:12; Acts 28:17–31

Thus said the Lord of hosts, "Truly, one who touches you touches the apple of my eye." Zechariah 2:8

Amazing grace, how can it be 77s*
that God to us is true,
that we are precious in God's sight,
despite the things we do?
Creator, former, shaper,
 making real what we have known,
that God's love is dependable,
and names us as God's own.

Just as you did it to one of the least of these who are members of my family, you did it to me. Matthew 25:40

Won't you walk with me, Jesus, 87s**
down the long road of life?
Won't you walk with me, Jesus, all the way?
I keep seeing you in others,
in my sisters, in my brothers;
help me reach out, O Jesus, on my way.

Creator of the universe, it is amazing that we mortal creatures—every one of us—are precious to you. Even more, you tell us that we meet you through one another. Plant and nurture in us the faith to believe and to live by those amazing truths. Amen.

Tuesday, March 7 — Psalm 33:12–22
Ezra 6:13–7:28; Romans 1:1–12

The Lord our God may not leave us or abandon us. 1 Kings 8:57

As a mother holds her baby, 659
gazing in her child's eyes
with a look of deep connection,
pond'ring still unbroken ties,
so God looks into our faces
with a gaze so close and calm,
holding us against the body
out of which our life has come.

May the Lord direct your hearts to the love of God and to the steadfastness of Christ. 2 Thessalonians 3:5

As a mother looks with favor 659
on the new life in her arms,
searching ev'ry small expression,
sav'ring moments filled with charm,
so God smiles on ev'ry person,
so God takes such keen delight
in the praises that we offer;
we are precious in God's sight.

Faithful One, so many in our world feel abandoned and forgotten. When we are tempted to abandon or forget those in need, whether near or far away, we remember the love of parents for their children, a gift that reflects your faithfulness, and we give you thanks. Amen.

Wednesday, March 8 — Psalm 34:1–7
Ezra 8:1–20; Romans 1:13–25

O land, land, land, hear the word of the Lord! Jeremiah 22:29

Through the decades, driv'n by changes, *
farm to city, fam'lies strewn,
weak our roots, if farmland only:
sure foundation God alone.
Lord, may we, your body scattered,
find in you our life and home.

What you hear in the ear, preach on the housetops. Matthew 10:27 NKJV

Spread the care in which you hold us: *
this our goal, where'er we are;
in our life alone, together,
in our fam'ly and afar.
Though we, too, are hurt and wounded,
use us, Christ, like you, to heal.

Welcoming God, we all want a home, a place that is ours, that we can find on a map. But the scattering of friends and family reminds us of what has always been true: our only real home is in you. May we live by this, and be people who welcome and who heal. Amen.

* Written by Hermann Weinlick (1978) for Goshen [ND] centennial.

Thursday, March 9 — Psalm 34:8–18
Ezra 8:21–10:6; Romans 1:26–2:4

The Lord your God has been with you; you have lacked nothing. Deuteronomy 2:7

You make us rejoice in serving, 622*
giving strength where we had none;
certain tasks had seemed unnerving,
but you've proven you're the one
who gives gifts of love and power,
confidence and self-control.
Fill us now, this very hour;
help us reach your kingdom's goal.

Jesus said to his disciples, "When I sent you out without a purse, bag, or sandals, did you lack anything?" They said, "No, not a thing." Luke 22:35

You're our strength and motivation, 622*
Christ, you send us out to serve.
We hold back, but your salvation
gives us energy and nerve.
You still fill us with your Spirit;
lift us up on eagle's wings.
Give your call, we gladly hear it;
in your work our spirit sings.

Our Strength and Motivation, so much in the world needs to be replaced or fixed that we are overwhelmed. Lead us to some corner of life where, empowered by you, we may make a real difference and get a glimpse of your kingdom. Amen.

* Darryl Bell.

Friday, March 10 — Psalm 34:19–22
Ezra 10:7–44; Romans 2:5–16

He who keeps Israel will neither slumber nor sleep. Psalm 121:4

What God's almighty pow'r has made, 537
in mercy he is keeping;
by morning glow or evening shade
his eye is never sleeping.
And where he rules in kingly might,
there all is just and all is right:
to God all praise and glory!

Cast all your anxiety on him, because he cares for you. 1 Peter 5:7

Have we trials and temptations? 743
Is there trouble anywhere?
We should never be discouraged;
take it to the Lord in prayer!
Can we find a friend so faithful
who will all our sorrows share?
Jesus knows our ev'ry weakness;
take it to the Lord in prayer!

Ever-present Help and Stay, we tire; we grow weary; we want to rest. Give us the strength to live well this day and serve you faithfully this day. In Jesus' name, we pray. Amen.

Saturday, March 11 — Psalm 35:1–10
Nehemiah 1:1–2:10; Romans 2:17–3:2

Moses said, "See, I am setting before you today a blessing and a curse: the blessing, if you obey the commandments of the Lord your God that I am commanding you today; and the curse, if you do not obey the commandments of the Lord your God." Deuteronomy 11:26-28

God is waiting for us all 57s*
to wake up from our sleep.
If we'd only hear the call
such love we would receive.

Jesus said, "If you keep my commandments, you will abide in my love." John 15:10

Love will find you 57s*
if you'll open up your heart and let it in, let it in;
love will find you.
Won't you open up your life so love comes in,
love comes in?
It'll come in.

Loving God, you have created us so that you can bless us, but sometimes we resist. Sometimes we think of your commandments as roadblocks, not as guardrails on the road. Help us to discover the joy and satisfaction of obeying you. Amen.

Third Sunday in Lent

Watchword for the week — O come, let us worship and bow down, let us kneel before the Lord, our Maker! Psalm 95:6

Sunday, March 12 — Exodus 17:1-7; Psalm 95
Romans 5:1-11; John 4:5-42

The Lord your God will make you most prosperous in all the work of your hands. Deuteronomy 30:9 NIV

Visions of glory, visions triumphant, 81s*
bright wonders dance, Lord, charming our eyes;
yet, Lord, you call us to humble service,
doing your will, Lord, in the real world.

It is God who is at work in you, enabling you both to will and to work for his good pleasure. Philippians 2:13

Jesus, yourself to us reveal. p204
Grant that we may not only feel
some drawings of your grace,
but in communion with you live,
and daily from your death derive
the needful strength to run our race.

Source of all riches, what is prosperity? Visions of glory? Power? Getting what we want? Rather, help us to see that it is cooperating with you to make the best use of what you have given us for living lives pleasing to you. Amen.

* C. Daniel Crews (1999). © 2013 by IBOC and MMF.

Monday, March 13 — Psalm 35:11–18
Nehemiah 2:11–3:32; Romans 3:3–18

Why should the nations say, "Where is their God?" Our God is in the heavens; he does whatever he pleases. Psalm 115:2-3

This is my Father's world, 456
and to my list'ning ears
all nature sings and round me rings
the music of the spheres.
This is my Father's world;
I rest me in the thought
of rocks and trees, of skies and seas—
his hand the wonders wrought.

While God has overlooked the times of human ignorance, now he commands all people everywhere to repent. Acts 17:30

This is our Father's world: 456
O let us not forget
that though the wrong is often strong,
God is the ruler yet.
He trusts us with his world,
to keep it clean and fair—
all earth and trees, all skies and seas,
all creatures ev'rywhere.

Creator of all things, we give you thanks for the wonderful planet you have given us. In many ways, we have not cared for it well. Help us to repent and make the difficult choices to better care for our planet. Amen.

Tuesday, March 14 — Psalm 35:19–28
Nehemiah 4; Romans 3:19–31

I am coming to gather all nations and tongues; and they shall come and shall see my glory. Isaiah 66:18

All people that on earth do dwell, 539
sing to the Lord with cheerful voice;
serve him with joy, his praises tell,
come now before him and rejoice.

God, who said, "Let light shine out of darkness," made his light shine in our hearts to give us the light of the knowledge of God's glory displayed in the face of Christ. 2 Corinthians 4:6 NIV

Just as I am, weak flesh and mind; 44s*
sometimes my soul to you is blind,
but now, this day, I search, I find.
O Jesus, friend, I come, I come.

Jesus, light of the world, amid both the gaudy lights and the dark corners of this life, we need a sense of glory—especially the glory we see in you. And when we see that glory, may that glory, that light, shine through us. Amen.

* Willard R. Harstine (2009). © 2013 by IBOC and MMF.

Wednesday, March 15 — Psalm 36
Nehemiah 5:1–6:14; Romans 4:1–12

Great is his steadfast love toward us, and the faithfulness of the Lord endures forever. Praise the Lord! Psalm 117:2

A new psalm to the Lord now sing, 17s*
a song of thanks and praise,
for mercies beyond numbering
and courage for these days.

Blessed be the God and Father of our Lord Jesus Christ, the Father of mercies and the God of all consolation. 2 Corinthians 1:3

When foes without and fears within 17s*
and cares upon us weigh,
God, who our strength and shield has been,
will help us still today.

Eternal God, you endure forever. How can we mortals understand that? We thank you for our Lord Jesus Christ, whose resurrection and continuing life among us give us a taste of "forever." Amen.

* Carl Helmich, Jr. (2010). © 2013 by IBOC and MMF.

Thursday, March 16 — Psalm 37:1–6
Nehemiah 6:15–7:73a; Romans 4:13–25

He guarded his people as the apple of his eye. Deuteronomy 32:10

I love your church, O God! 513
Her walls before you stand,
dear as the apple of your eye,
and graven on your hand.

God is love, and those who abide in love abide in God, and God abides in them. 1 John 4:16

Thy nature, gracious Lord, impart; 477r
come quickly from above;
write thy new name upon my heart,
thy new, best name of love.

Loving God, we are "the apple of your eye"—a gift, not a reward for anything we have done. May that gift so shape us that we are indeed lovers of both strangers and our neighbors, especially those whom the world ignores or forgets. Amen.

Friday, March 17 — Psalm 37:7–15
Nehemiah 7:73b–8:18; Romans 5:1–11

O Lord, do your eyes not look for truth? Jeremiah 5:3

Lord, through changing days, unchanging, 435r
thou the light our fathers knew,
through our wid'ning ways, far ranging,
let thy splendor claim us too;
go beside us, lead and guide us
to whatever things are true.

Whoever is faithful in a very little is faithful also in much; and whoever is dishonest in a very little is dishonest also in much. Luke 16:10

Past all sham of small succeeding 435r
sordid gains that call and woo,
lift us by the mighty leading
fit for thine aspiring few;
hold us serving, all unswerving,
whatsoever things are true.

Ever-living God, surrounded by changes and falsehoods, we often doubt that anything is true or dependable. Enable us to trust you as the truth upon which we can rely, so that we may be faithful people. Amen.

Saturday, March 18 — Psalm 37:16–22
Nehemiah 9:1–10:27; Romans 5:12–6:4

They have all gone astray, they are all alike perverse; there is no one who does good, no, not one. Psalm 14:3

Lord, have mercy upon my soul; 48s*
the war within seems out of control.
Take this bitterness and turn it into gratefulness.
Lord, have mercy upon my soul.

For the gate is narrow and the road is hard that leads to life, and there are few who find it. Matthew 7:14

Spirit, fill me with your strength; 48s*
my own resolve will fail me at length.
Set my spirit free to wait upon you patiently.
Spirit, fill me with your strength.

Lord God, your way is not easy. It is narrow. But despite our failures and our going astray, your way is what you have made us for, and what leads us to genuine life. Amen.

Fourth Sunday in Lent

Watchword for the week — Surely goodness and mercy shall follow me all the days of my life, and I shall dwell in the house of the Lord my whole life long. Psalm 23:6

Sunday, March 19 — 1 Samuel 16:1-13; Psalm 23
Ephesians 5:8-14; John 9:1-41

There is no holy one like the Lord, no one besides you. 1 Samuel 2:2

O Lord and Master of us all, 479r
whate'er our name or sign,
we own thy sway, we hear thy call,
and test our lives by thine.

As he who called you is holy, be holy yourselves in all your conduct. 1 Peter 1:15

May it in our walk be seen 586
that we have with Jesus been,
that as king o'er us he reigns
and unrivaled pow'r maintains.

Divine Companion, we are shaped by the company we keep. We need your company, so touch us that we may know we have been with you and have been changed. Amen.

Monday, March 20 — Psalm 37:23–26
Nehemiah 10:28–11:36; Romans 6:5–16

Come, let us walk in the light of the Lord! Isaiah 2:5

What splendid rays of truth and grace, 596
all other light excelling!
This I know when he in love
makes my heart his dwelling!

Jesus said, "I am the light of the world. Whoever follows me will never walk in darkness but will have the light of life." John 8:12

Light of the world, you are the way; 38s*
to you ourselves we give,
to share your death on this dark day,
and by your light to live.

Jesus, every morning's sunrise reminds us that you are the light of the world. It is easy to be discouraged by the darkness. Open our eyes to see the light and in some small way to be the light for others as we follow you. Amen.

Tuesday, March 21 — Psalm 37:27–33
Nehemiah 12:1–43; Romans 6:17–7:6

One does not live by bread alone, but by every word that comes from the mouth of the Lord. Deuteronomy 8:3

> We would not live by bread alone, 411
> but by your word of grace,
> in strength of which we travel on
> to our abiding place.

Lord, to whom can we go? You have the words of eternal life. John 6:68

> Be known to us in breaking bread, 411
> but do not then depart;
> Savior, abide with us, and spread
> your table in our heart.

Bread of life, we often prefer to dine on the fast foods of the world around us. Convert our appetites. Make us hungry for real food. Make us hungry for you, the feast that nourishes and satisfies. Amen.

Wednesday, March 22 — Psalm 37:34–40
Nehemiah 12:44–13:14; Romans 7:7–20

I will seek the lost, and I will bring back the strayed. I will bind up the injured, and I will strengthen the weak. Ezekiel 34:16

Lost am I from God my maker, 19s*
lost in darkness and despair,
like a coin dropped from a pocket
in a corner, under chair.
Will God seek me? Will God find me?
Or long silence must I bear?

Jesus said, "When the shepherd comes home, he calls together his friends and neighbors, saying to them, 'Rejoice with me, for I have found my sheep that was lost.'" Luke 15:6

Lord you make our hearts rejoice, 662**
we're your sheep and know your voice.
You're our shepherd, kind and gracious,
and your pastures are delicious;
constant love to us you show,
yea, our very names you know.

Good Shepherd, sometimes we are lost and yearn to be found. More often, we don't even know we are lost. Help us to know the joy of being found by you. Amen.

** adapted.

Thursday, March 23 — Psalm 38:1–8
Nehemiah 13:15–31; Romans 7:21–8:8

You silence the roaring of the seas, the tumult of the peoples. Psalm 65:7

Drop thy still dews of quietness 373r
till all our strivings cease.
Take from our souls the strain and stress;
and let our ordered lives confess
the beauty of thy peace.

Zechariah said, "With a solemn oath to our ancestor Abraham the God of Israel promised to rescue us from our enemies and allow us to serve him without fear all the days of our life." Luke 1:73-75 GNT

The faithful waited long 36s*
for God to intervene,
to rule with pow'r and might,
to give them what they dreamed.
What a big surprise!
The Savior was a child!
The Christmas story goes to show
God's plans are really wild!

Jesus, quiet friend, we are usually impressed by speed and noise and power. You invite us to your wild and different ways: of listening, humility, and compassion. Lead us in that way. Amen.

Friday, March 24 — Psalm 38:9–16
Esther 1; Romans 8:9–19

Thus says the Lord, I myself have spoken to you persistently, and you have not obeyed me. Jeremiah 35:14

When human passions blind the mind, 64s*
and fearfulness might rule the day,
when on this earth no hope we find,
be then our only hope and stay.

Jesus said, "Blessed are those who hear the word of God and keep it!" Luke 11:28 NKJV

As we go forth to do your will, 64s*
Lord, guide us, and your word fulfill,
and show us how to work and be
your blessed disciples, wholly free.

Our Hope and Stay, on our own, we fall far short of your hopes for us. We go our own way. We live fearful lives. But when we really are open to your guidance, we know that we are blessed. Thank you. Amen.

* st. 2 by C. Daniel Crews; st. 4 by John A. Craver (2006).

Saturday, March 25 — Psalm 38:17–22
Esther 2:1–18; Romans 8:20–33

One who is slow to anger is better than the mighty and one whose temper is controlled than one who captures a city. Proverbs 16:32

We're called to take the risky step, 77s*
align with those in need,
to vision the new thing God's doing
within community.
The challenge is to not rely on raw reality
that shrouds our hope,
obscuring all that God would have us see.

Blessed are the peacemakers, for they will be called children of God. Matthew 5:9

[God's] river flows for all the world, 77s*
and as God's own we are
the means of grace and love to heal
the wounds and mend the scars.
God's love that stirred our church back then,
still moves our church today,
Creator, former, shaper, bringing new,
transforming ways.

Peacemaking God, you call us to live differently: controlling temper, seeking community, being able to take the risky step. You call us to be a means of your grace. Show us how wonderful and exciting it can be to live as your peacemaking children. Amen.

Fifth Sunday in Lent

Watchword for the week — I wait for the Lord, my soul waits, and in his word I hope. Psalm 130:5

Sunday, March 26 — Ezekiel 37:1-14; Psalm 130
Romans 8:6-11; John 11:1-45

Solomon said at the dedication of the temple, "Will God indeed dwell on the earth?" 1 Kings 8:27

We long for mighty signs of God, p58*
cathedral, miracle, and sword,
his power and glory written plain
so none may doubt that he is Lord.

No one has ever seen God. It is God the only Son, who is close to the Father's heart, who has made him known. John 1:18

But poor in weakness comes the Christ; p58*
his glory gone, no king we see;
a servant Lord, no praise he seeks.
thus comes God's power to you and me.

Invisible God, we long to see you; we need to see you on the earth. Invisible God, you have become visible in Jesus—but not as we expected. Invisible God, may what we see in Jesus, especially forgiveness and service, be reflected in us. Amen.

Monday, March 27 — Psalm 39:1–6
Esther 2:19–3:15; Romans 8:34–9:7

Your name, O God, like your praise, reaches to the ends of the earth. Psalm 48:10

Before Jehovah's glorious throne, 160r
ye nations, bow with sacred joy;
know that the Lord is God alone;
he can create and he destroy.

Jesus said, "As you go, proclaim the good news, 'The kingdom of heaven has come near.'" Matthew 10:7

Enter his gates with thankful songs, 160r
and in his courts your voices raise.
Let earth, with her ten thousand tongues,
sound forth, almighty Lord, thy praise.

Great Musician, you have made us, as people created in your image, to sing. We sing because we are alive. We sing because, whatever our circumstances, life is good. We sing because, in Jesus, we have a glimpse of your kingdom. We sing because we are your people. Hallelujah! Amen.

Tuesday, March 28 — Psalm 39:7–13
Esther 4,5; Romans 9:8–21

He knows how we were made; he remembers that we are dust. Psalm 103:14

Frail children of dust, and feeble as frail, 158r
in thee do we trust, nor find thee to fail;
thy mercies how tender, how firm to the end,
our Maker, Defender, Redeemer, and Friend.

We always carry around in our body the death of Jesus, so that the life of Jesus may also be revealed in our body. 2 Corinthians 4:10 NIV

Risen Christ, redeem our life, 32s*
as we take up our own cross,
work and pray and sacrifice
to advance your kingdom's cause.

Giver of life, we are dust, and to dust we shall return. But we are more than dust. We give you thanks for Jesus' promise of new life, both in our present mortal bodies and after we are again dust. Praise be to you. Amen.

* Carl Helmich, Jr. (2011).

Wednesday, March 29 — Psalm 40:1–8
Esther 6,7; Romans 9:22–33

Praise the Lord, all you nations! Extol him, all you peoples! Psalm 117:1

God is love; and love enfolds us, 463
all the world in one embrace;
with unfailing grasp God holds us,
ev'ry child of ev'ry race.
And when human hearts are breaking
under sorrow's iron rod,
then we find that self-same aching
deep within the heart of God.

On the Day of Pentecost the people said, "We hear them speaking in our own tongues the wonderful works of God." Acts 2:11 NKJV

Church, go forth o'er the earth; 631
Christ, your head, has hallowed you,
a chosen bride forever,
adorned now for our Savior;
be strong and be not cheerless,
and may your saints be fearless;
in all places, with all races,
may that story of his glory
be the hope of all the world.

Holy Spirit, on Pentecost, you demonstrated your desire to bring together all nations. Yet we humans seem intent on growing divisions and hate. May we, who bear the name of Jesus, so live that we show the world your love for all and your desire for harmony among people. Amen.

Thursday, March 30 — Psalm 40:9–17
Esther 8:1–9:17; Romans 10:1–13

For everything there is a season, and a time for every matter under heaven. Ecclesiastes 3:1

If the way be drear, 799
if the foe be near,
let no faithless fears o'ertake us,
let not faith and hope forsake us;
safely past the foe
to our home we go.

Then Jesus took the twelve aside and said to them, "See, we are going up to Jerusalem, and everything that is written about the Son of Man by the prophets will be accomplished." Luke 18:31

For he, my soul has sent his Son p72
to die for wrongs which you have done;
he paid the ransom, and forgives
the hourly follies of our lives.

Jesus, divine and human leader, whatever the season—hard or easy, surprising or expected, with destination clear or unknown—you both lead us and go with us. Strengthen our often-feeble wills to trust your leadership. Amen.

Friday, March 31 — Psalm 41
Esther 9:18–10:3; Romans 10:14–11:6

When the Israelites cried out to the Lord, the Lord raised up a deliverer, who delivered them. Judges 3:9

Call Jehovah your salvation, 176r
rest beneath the Almighty's shade;
in his secret habitation
dwell, nor ever be dismayed;
there no tumult can alarm you,
you shall dread no hidden snare;
guile nor violence can harm you
in eternal safeguard there.

Zechariah said, "Blessed be the Lord God of Israel, for he has looked favorably on his people and redeemed them." Luke 1:68

As we are taught of Jesus 434*
we celebrate the faith
built up by those before us
and passed through us today.
Thus our lives are established
in time and history.
We know who we are called to be:
The church, empow'red in ministry
to serve all people lovingly.
Alleluia!

Savior, from what do we need to be saved or delivered? Turn our attention from the foes outside us to the foes within us. Turn our eyes from the faults of others to see our own faults. Help us to find our salvation in turning from self-centered ways and in joyfully living as your own people. Amen.

Saturday, April 1 — Psalm 42
Job 1,2; Romans 11:7–18

The Lord will not cast away his people, for his great name's sake. 1 Samuel 12:22

As a parent's love is endless, 534*
so God's mercy follows us;
for the Lord who framed our being
well recalls that we are dust!

If we are faithless, he remains faithful—for he cannot deny himself. 2 Timothy 2:13

O God, my faithful God, 615
O fountain ever flowing,
without whom nothing is,
all perfect gifts bestowing,
grant me a faithful life,
and give me, Lord, within,
commitment free from strife,
a soul unhurt by sin.

So many times, God, we have turned away from you, giving you every reason to turn away from us. Yet, patiently and persistently, you pull us back from our pride and selfishness. You labor to restore us to yourself and to one another. Thank you, faithful God. Amen.

Palm Sunday

Watchword for the week — And being found in human form, Jesus humbled himself and became obedient to the point of death—even death on a cross. Philippians 2:7,8

Sunday, April 2 — Isaiah 50:4-9a; Psalm 31:9-16
Philippians 2:5-11; Matthew 21:1-11

I will turn their mourning into joy. Jeremiah 31:13

Joyful, joyful, we adore you, 544
God of glory, Lord of love;
hearts unfold like flow'rs before you,
op'ning to the sun above.
Melt the clouds of sin and sadness;
drive the dark of doubt away;
giver of immortal gladness,
fill us with the light of day!

Jesus said, "Blessed are those who mourn, for they will be comforted." Matthew 5:4

"Comfort, comfort now my people; 264
tell of peace!" So says our God.
Comfort those who sit in darkness
bowed beneath oppression's load.
To God's people now proclaim
that God's pardon waits for them!
Tell them that their war is over;
God will reign in peace forever!

Jesus of Nazareth, as you rode into Jerusalem, ride into our hearts today. Hear us as we shout, "Blessed is the One who comes in the name of the Lord." Let us bless you even as you bless and comfort us with freedom, purpose, and joy. Amen.

Monday, April 3 — Psalm 43
Job 3,4; Romans 11:19–32

I keep my eyes always on the Lord. Psalm 16:8 NIV

Be thou my vision, O Lord of my heart; 719
nought be all else to me save that thou art—
thou my best thought, by day or by night,
waking or sleeping, thy presence my light.

Let us look to Jesus, the pioneer and perfecter of our faith, who for the sake of the joy that was set before him endured the cross, disregarding its shame. Hebrews 12:2

Consecrate me now to thy service, Lord, 607
by the pow'r of grace divine;
let my soul look up with a steadfast hope
and my will be lost in thine.

When our eyes wander from you, Lord, we see only the brokenness of human striving and despair. Yet, even on that bleak horizon, we also see your arms stretched out on the cross. We see you, Lord, beginning and ending everything with love. Amen.

Tuesday, April 4 — Psalm 44:1–8
Job 5,6; Romans 11:33–12:8

Fear not, O land; Be glad and rejoice, for the Lord has done marvelous things! Joel 2:21 NKJV

Lift ev'ry voice and sing, 707
till earth and heaven ring,
ring with the harmonies of liberty.
Let our rejoicing rise
high as the list'ning skies,
let it resound loud as the rolling sea.
Sing a song full of the faith
that the dark past has taught us.
Sing a song full of the hope
that the present has brought us.
Facing the rising sun
of our new day begun,
let us march on till victory is won.

The whole multitude of the disciples began to praise God joyfully with a loud voice for all the deeds of power that they had seen, saying, "Blessed is the king who comes in the name of the Lord!" Luke 19:37-38

Fling wide the door, unbar the gate; 272*
the King of glory comes in state,
the Lord of lords and King of kings,
the Savior of the world who brings
his great salvation to the earth.
So raise a shout of holy mirth
and praise our God and Lord,
Creator, Spirit, Word.

We lift up our loud voices. We praise and welcome you, Lord. We give thanks because you ride boldly into our lives, our cities, and nations. You bring health, healing, and hope that God's mercy and justice will prevail in the world around us. Amen.

Wednesday, April 5 — Psalm 44:9–16
Job 7; Romans 12:9–21

The Lord loves righteousness and justice. Psalm 33:5

Pray justice may come rolling down 696*
as in a mighty stream,
with righteousness in field and town
to cleanse us and redeem.
For God is longing to restore
an earth where conflicts cease,
a world that was created for
a harmony of peace.

You know the generous act of our Lord Jesus Christ, that though he was rich, yet for your sakes he became poor, so that by his poverty you might become rich. 2 Corinthians 8:9

He left his Father's throne above— 773
so free, so infinite his grace—
emptied himself of all but love,
and bled for Adam's helpless race!
What mercy this, immense and free,
for, O my God, it found out me!
What mercy this, immense and free,
for, O my God, it found out me!

Thank you, justice-loving God. Seeing our hungry bodies and empty hearts, you give us your commandments and show us the way to live in harmony with one another. Knowing we need still more, you show us that self-sacrificing love—yours and ours—enriches your world with mercy and peace. Amen.

Maundy Thursday

Maundy Thursday — He has gained renown by his wonderful deeds; the Lord is gracious and merciful. Psalm 111:4

Thursday, April 6 — Psalm 44:17–26
Job 8; Romans 13

God said, "As long as the earth endures, seedtime and harvest, cold and heat, summer and winter, day and night, shall not cease." Genesis 8:22

Summer and winter, 460*
and springtime and harvest,
sun, moon, and stars in their courses above
join with all nature in manifold witness
to thy great faithfulness, mercy, and love.

Jesus took a loaf of bread, and when he had given thanks, he broke it and gave it to them, saying, "This is my body, which is given for you. Do this in remembrance of me." And he did the same with the cup after supper, saying, "This cup that is poured out for you is the new covenant in my blood." Luke 22:19-20

Lord, as round this feast we gather, p187**
fill our hearts with holy rapture!
For this bread and cup of blessing
are for us the sure possessing
of your loving deed on Calv'ry,
of your living self, our vict'ry,
pledge of your unfailing presence,
foretaste here of heav'nly gladness.

As faithful as the cycles of day and night, and seedtime and harvest may be, you, Lord, are even more faithful. You invite us again and again to your table as treasured guests. We give thanks, fully and freely without end, that you give yourself to us in love. Amen.

Good Friday

Good Friday — For God so loved the world that he gave his only Son, so that everyone who believes in him may not perish but may have eternal life. John 3:16

Friday, April 7 — Psalm 45:1–9
Job 9; Romans 14:1–12

O taste and see that the Lord is good; happy are those who take refuge in him. Psalm 34:8

Lift ev'ry voice and sing, 707
till earth and heaven ring,
ring with the harmonies of liberty.
Let our rejoicing rise
high as the list'ning skies,
let it resound loud as the rolling sea.
Sing a song full of the faith
  that the dark past has taught us.
Sing a song full of the hope
  that the present has brought us.
Facing the rising sun
of our new day begun
let us march on till victory is won.

One of the criminals said, "Jesus, remember me when you come into your kingdom." He replied, "Truly I tell you, today you will be with me in Paradise." Luke 23:42-43

Amen, yea, my lasting praises, 808
Jesus, unto you are giv'n,
that a place by you prepared
is for me secured in heav'n;
blessed my case, O truly blessed,
when to heav'nly glory raised,
I from pain and sorrow free
in your presence safe shall be.

Christ, even as we see you hang upon the cross, we pray a humble, earnest plea. May we savor the taste of your forgiveness and the sweetness of your love in this life and in the life yet to come. Amen.

Great Sabbath

Saturday, April 8 — Psalm 45:10–17
Job 10; Romans 14:13–15:2

The Lord drew me up from the desolate pit, out of the miry bog, and set my feet upon a rock, making my steps secure. Psalm 40:2

Faithful soul, pray, always pray, 729
and still in God confide;
he your stumbling steps shall stay,
and shall not let you slide;
safe from known or secret foes,
free from sin and Satan's hold,
when the flesh, earth, hell oppose,
he'll keep you in his fold.

Christ was put to death in the flesh, but made alive in the spirit, in which also he went and made a proclamation to the spirits in prison. 1 Peter 3:18-19

Great God, in Christ you set us free 579*
your life to live, your joy to share.
Give us your Spirit's liberty
to turn from guilt and dull despair
and offer all that faith can do
while love is making all things new.

Jesus, when we are in prison, entombed in the consequences of our own sin, speak to us words of hope. Pull us up, set us free. Place our feet securely on the solid rock of your love. Amen.

Easter Sunday

Watchword for the week — So if you have been raised with Christ, seek the things that are above, where Christ is, seated at the right hand of God. Colossians 3:1

Sunday, April 9 — Acts 10:34-43; Psalm 118:1-2,14-24
Colossians 3:1-4; John 20:1-18

I lie down and sleep; I wake again, for the Lord sustains me. Psalm 3:5

> Lord, may I be at rest in you 569
> and sweetly sleep the whole night through.
> Refresh my strength for your own sake,
> so I may serve you when I wake.

After Jesus rose early on the first day of the week, he appeared first to Mary Magdalene, from whom he had cast out seven demons. She went out and told those who had been with him, while they were mourning and weeping. Mark 16:9-10

> Go spread the news, he's not in the grave. 357*
> He has arisen, the world to save.
> Jesus' redeeming labors are done.
> Even the battle with sin is won.

Refreshed by sleep, help us rise to live a new day. With eyes that see more clearly in morning's light, help us, Lord, to recognize Christ alive among us, bringing us hope and purpose. May we, like Mary, tell those still weary with night's mourning, "Christ is risen! Alleluia." Amen.

Monday, April 10 — Psalm 46
Job 11:1–12:12; Romans 15:3–16

The Lord will fight for you, and you have only to keep still. Exodus 14:14

Be still my soul: the Lord is on your side. 757
Bear patiently the cross of grief or pain;
leave to your God to order and provide;
in ev'ry change God faithful will remain.
Be still, my soul: your best, your heav'nly friend
through thorny ways leads to a joyful end.

Thanks be to God, who gives us the victory through our Lord Jesus Christ. 1 Corinthians 15:57

True God, he first from death has burst 368*
forth into life, all subduing.
His enemy shall vanquished lie;
his death has been death's undoing.
"And yours shall be like victory
o'er death and grave," said he, who gave
his life for us, life renewing.

Life's enemies threaten—poverty, sickness, disaster, doubt, death. Let me hide behind you, defender God, as you battle them on my behalf. Let my troubled soul be still, trusting that your love and mercy will prevail, protecting me and the whole of your creation. Amen.

Tuesday, April 11 — Psalm 47
Job 12:13–13:19; Romans 15:17–29

You have made the Lord your refuge. Psalm 91:9

The Lord is never far away, 537
but through all grief distressing,
an everpresent help and stay,
our peace, and joy, and blessing.
As with a mother's tender hand,
he leads his own, his chosen band.
To God all praise and glory!

For just as the sufferings of Christ are abundant for us, so also our consolation is abundant through Christ. 2 Corinthians 1:5

Who trusts in God, a strong abode p121*
in heav'n and earth possesses;
who looks in love to Christ above,
no fear the heart oppresses.
In you alone, dear Lord, we own
sweet hope and consolation,
our shield from foes, our balm for woes,
our great and sure salvation.

Protector God, when fierce storms threaten, you give us shelter and refuge under your wings like a mother hen. You murmur comforting words of consolation that all will be well. We give thanks that you care for us and raise us up, even as you cared for and raised up Christ. Amen.

* Lehoma Goode.

Wednesday, April 12 — Psalm 48
Job 13:20–14:22; Romans 15:30–16:7

I—My hands—stretched out the heavens, and all their host I have commanded. Isaiah 45:12 NKJV

We sing your mighty power, O God, *
that made the mountains rise,
that spread the flowing seas abroad,
and built the lofty skies.
We sing the wisdom that ordained
the sun to rule the day;
the moon shines full at your command,
and all the stars obey.

Every generous act of giving, with every perfect gift, is from above, coming down from the Father of lights, with whom there is no variation or shadow due to change. James 1:17

God, whose giving knows no ending, 652**
from your rich and endless store;
nature's wonder, Jesus' wisdom,
costly cross, grave's shattered door,
gifted by you, we turn to you,
off'ring up ourselves in praise;
thankful song shall rise forever,
gracious donor of our days.

As energy streams from the sun, giving light and food to the earth, so even the universe itself, with all its light and love, streams from you, creator God. May your creative energy be the source of our own gifts in return: caring for and revering creation. Amen.

* by Isaac Watts. Public Domain.

Thursday, April 13 — Psalm 49:1–12
Job 15,16; Romans 16:8–20

Lord, in your great mercies you did not make an end of your people or forsake them. Nehemiah 9:31

O bless the Lord, my soul! 546
His mercies bear in mind!
Forget not all his benefits!
The Lord to all is kind.
He pardons all our sins,
prolongs our feeble breath;
he heals all our infirmities
and ransoms us from death.

Jesus said, "Because I live, you also will live." John 14:19

God sent his Son, they called him Jesus, 706
he came to love, heal, and forgive;
he lived and died to buy my pardon,
an empty grave is there to prove my Savior lives.

In a world full of negative "becauses" that lead to despair and isolation, thank you, God, for being the loving "because" that leads us to hope and community. Give us the "because" that we need today to live as your people, working for your justice and peace. Amen.

Friday, April 14 — Psalm 49:13–20
Job 17,18; Romans 16:21–1 Corinthians 1:1–9

The days are surely coming, says the Lord, when I will raise up for David a righteous branch, and he shall reign as king and deal wisely, and shall execute justice and righteousness in the land. Jeremiah 23:5

Hail to the Lord's anointed! 263
Great David's greater Son!
Hail, in the time appointed,
his reign on earth begun!
He comes to break oppression,
to set the captive free,
to take away transgression,
and rule in equity.

Jesus set free those who were slaves all their lives because of their fear of death. Hebrews 2:15 GNT

Long my imprisoned spirit lay 773
fast bound in sin and nature's night.
Your sunrise turned that night to day;
I woke—the dungeon flamed with light!
My chains fell off, your voice I knew;
was freed, I rose, and followed you.
My chains fell off, your voice I knew;
was freed, I rose, and followed you.

Son of David, just and kind ruler, set us free from the prisons and chains of our own and other's making. Release us from poverty to enjoy your abundance. Release us from guilt to experience forgiveness. Release us from despair to live with hope and purpose. Amen.

Saturday, April 15 — Psalm 50:1–6
Job 19; 1 Corinthians 1:10–20

God is wise in heart, and mighty in strength— who has resisted him, and succeeded? Job 9:4

Immortal, invisible, God only wise, 457
in light inaccessible hid from our eyes,
most blessed, most glorious, O Ancient of Days,
almighty, victorious, your great name we praise.

But who indeed are you, a human being, to argue with God? Romans 9:20

God the all-righteous one! Earth has defied you, *
yet to eternity stands what you say;
falsehood and wrong shall not tarry beside you;
give to us peace in our time, we pray.

We resist, Lord. We argue; we think we know best. We lead ourselves into cold, dangerous, empty places. Help us instead, wise and compassionate God, to listen to your voice, take your hand, and journey where you lead into warm, safe places of peace and freedom. Amen.

* by Henry F. Chorley (1842). Public Domain.

Second Sunday of Easter

Watchword of the week — Blessed be the God and Father of our Lord Jesus Christ! By his great mercy he has given us a new birth into a living hope through the resurrection of Jesus Christ from the dead. 1 Peter 1:3

Sunday, April 16 — Acts 2:14a,22-32; Psalm 16
1 Peter 1:3-9; John 20:19-31

Extol the Lord our God; worship at his footstool. Holy is he! Psalm 99:5

Holy God, we praise your name: 386
Lord of all, we bow before you.
Saints on earth your rule acclaim;
all in heaven above adore you.
Infinite your vast domain;
everlasting is your reign.

When they had prayed, the place in which they were gathered together was shaken; and they were all filled with the Holy Spirit and spoke the word of God with boldness. Acts 4:31

O Spirit, sent from heaven 378*
on that day long ago,
rekindle faith among us
in all life's ebb and flow.
O give us ears to listen
and tongues aflame with praise,
so people of all nations
glad songs of joy shall raise.

Drawing strength from one another, we wait for you, Lord. Let your powerful Spirit move among us. Make us bold, not only to tell your story with words, but to live your story by feeding the hungry, healing the sick, caring for the land, and welcoming the stranger. Amen.

Monday, April 17 — Psalm 50:7–15
Job 20; 1 Corinthians 1:21–2:2

Remember the Lord in a distant land, and let Jerusalem come into your mind. Jeremiah 51:50

By the waters, *
the waters of Babylon
we sat down and wept,
and wept for Zion.
We remember,
we remember,
we remember, Zion.

So then you are no longer strangers and aliens, but you are citizens with the saints and also members of the household of God. Ephesians 2:19

Once you were an alien people, 526**
strangers to God's heart of love;
Christ has brought you home in mercy,
citizens of heav'n above;
let his love flow out to others,
let them feel the Savior's care;
that they too may know his welcome
and his countless blessings share.

Pandemic, division, fear, self-loathing—they threaten to exile us from one another and from you, merciful God. Bring us out from our places of isolation. Gather us into the home of your heart. No longer strangers, join us together as members of your beloved family. Amen.

* Traditional. Public Domain.

Tuesday, April 18 — Psalm 50:16–23
Job 21; 1 Corinthians 2:3–16

The king of Israel, the Lord, is in your midst; you shall fear disaster no more. Zephaniah 3:15

Lord, when the tempest rages, 791*
I need not fear;
for you, the Rock of Ages,
are always near.
Close by your side abiding,
I fear no foe,
for when your hand is guiding,
in peace I go.

God did not give us a spirit of cowardice, but rather a spirit of power and of love and of self-discipline. 2 Timothy 1:7

Lo! The hosts of evil round us 751**
scorn the Christ, assail his ways!
From the fears that long have bound us,
free our hearts to faith and praise.
Grant us wisdom, grant us courage,
for the living of these days,
for the living of these days.

Seeing the violent chaos of our human-making, Lord, you could justifiably wipe your hands of us and leave us cowering in fear. Instead, you offer us your powerful love. Give us wisdom to open our hearts to your Spirit and courage to follow where you lead. Amen.

Wednesday, April 19 — Psalm 51:1–6
Job 22,23; 1 Corinthians 3:1–11

I will save you that you may become a blessing. Zechariah 8:13 NASB

Blessed to be a blessing, 582*
privileged to care,
challenged by the need
apparent ev'rywhere,
where the world is wanting
fill the vacant place,
be the means through which the
Lord reveals his grace.

Not that we are competent of ourselves to claim anything as coming from us; our competence is from God. 2 Corinthians 3:5

My pow'r is faint and low 604
till I have learned to serve;
it lacks the needed fire to glow,
it lacks the breeze to nerve;
it cannot drive the world
until itself be driv'n;
its flag can only be unfurled
when you shall breathe from heav'n.

Save us, Lord, so that we too may be a blessing. Wash away our guilt, so that we may forgive. Heal us, so that we may alleviate pain. Fill us with hope and courage, so that we may offer a despairing world the light of your justice and love. Amen.

Thursday, April 20 — Psalm 51:7–12
Job 24; 1 Corinthians 3:12–23

The Lord said, "I will defend this city to save it, for my own sake." 2 Kings 19:34

God is my strong salvation, 769
no enemy I fear;
he hears my supplication,
dispelling all my care;
if he, my head and master,
defend me from above,
what pain or what disaster
can part me from his love?

Do not be afraid, little flock, for it is your Father's good pleasure to give you the kingdom. Luke 12:32

Rejoice, rejoice, the kingdom comes; 260*
be glad, for it is near.
It comes with joy surprising us;
it triumphs o'er our fears.
Give thanks, for as the kingdom comes
it brings God's own shalom,
a state of peace and justice
where all with God are one.

Defend us, Lord, from the self-delusions, doubts, and despairs that defy our hope in your coming kingdom. Cast away our fears. Gather us up gently. Reign over us with mercy and justice, so that every living thing may peacefully enjoy the abundance of your creation. Amen.

Friday, April 21 — Psalm 51:13–19
Job 25–27; 1 Corinthians 4:1–15

You shall not bear false witness against your neighbor. Exodus 20:16

Keep me from saying words 615
that later need recalling;
guard me, lest idle speech
may from my lips be falling;
but when, within my place,
I must and ought to speak,
then to my words give grace,
lest I offend the weak.

Let come out of your mouths what is useful for building up, as there is need, so that your words may give grace to those who hear. Ephesians 4:29

Lord, speak to me, that I may speak 646
in living echoes of your tone.
As you have sought, so let me seek
your erring children lost and lone.

God, the word who spoke creation into being, God, the word who teaches us how to love each other, make us value the power of our own words to create and encourage. Help us speak words of comfort and hope, truth and justice, joy and peace. Amen.

Saturday, April 22 — Psalm 52
Job 28; 1 Corinthians 4:16–5:8

Lord, let me know my end, and what is the measure of my days; let me know how fleeting my life is. Psalm 39:4

Lifegiving Creator of both great and small; 457
of all life the maker, the true life of all;
we blossom, then wither like leaves on the tree,
but you live forever who was and will be.

We know that if the earthly tent we live in is destroyed, we have a building from God, a house not made with hands, eternal in the heavens. 2 Corinthians 5:1

Life of freedom, gladness, truth, 363*
all our guilt and fear transcending,
life that leaps beyond the grave,
God's own life that knows no ending;
life eternal, gift unpriced,
freely ours in Jesus Christ!

My body, like a tent made with human hands, is transitory upon this earth. Fleeting, it will wither away into death. Reassure me, Lord, that in the resurrection you will provide for me a new body, a new dwelling, a new way of resting in your heart of love. Amen.

Third Sunday of Easter

Watchword for the week — You have been born anew, not of perishable but of imperishable seed, through the living and enduring word of God. 1 Peter 1:23

Sunday, April 23 — Acts 2:14a,36-41; Psalm 116:1-4,12-19
1 Peter 1:17-23; Luke 24:13-35

"Who can hide in secret places so that I cannot see them?" says the Lord. "Do I not fill heaven and earth?" Jeremiah 23:24

God, you fill up earth and heaven *
with your justice and your love;
nothing hides from your clear eyesight,
large or small, below, above.
God, you know our strength and weakness.
God, you know our joy and pain.
You alone can fairly judge us.

Before him no creature is hidden, but all are naked and laid bare to the eyes of the one to whom we must render an account. Hebrews 4:13

My Father, I have wandered 763**
and hidden from your face;
in foolishness have squandered
your legacy of grace.
But now, in exile dwelling,
I rise with fear and shame,
as distant but compelling,
I hear you call my name.

Full of pride, we avoid you. Fearing your demands, we evade you. Full of shame, we slip into shadows. And yet, searching God, we cannot hide from you. You never lose sight of us. In every time and place, you still seek to direct, support, console, and protect us. Amen.

Monday, April 24 — Psalm 53
Job 29; 1 Corinthians 5:9–6:8

My soul waits for the Lord more than those who watch for the morning. Psalm 130:6

My soul is waiting for the Lord 761*
as one who longs for morning;
no watcher waits with greater hope
than I for his returning.
I hope as Israel in the Lord;
he sends redemption through his word.
We praise him for his mercy.

Keep yourselves in the love of God; look forward to the mercy of our Lord Jesus Christ that leads to eternal life. Jude 21

Jesus, still lead on 799
till our rest be won;
heav'nly leader, still direct us,
still support, console, protect us,
till we safely stand
in the promised land.

In the quiet dark of night, we wait for the earth to make its trustworthy turn into day, for early gray dawn to light our way. We wait too for you, trustworthy God. In new morning light, help us live embraced by your love, motivated by your will. Amen.

Tuesday, April 25 — Psalm 54
Job 30; 1 Corinthians 6:9–20

Light shines in the darkness for the upright; [he is] gracious, compassionate, and righteous. Psalm 112:4 NASB

We are called to be God's people, 635*
showing by our lives his grace,
one in heart and one in spirit,
sign of hope for all the race.
Let us show how he has changed us,
and remade us as his own,
let us share our life together
as we shall around his throne.

This slight momentary affliction is preparing us for an eternal weight of glory beyond all measure, because we look not at what can be seen but at what cannot be seen. 2 Corinthians 4:17-18

God is love; and though with blindness 463
sin afflicts all human life,
God's eternal lovingkindness
guides us through our earthly strife.
Sin and death and hell shall never
o'er us final triumph gain:
God is love, so love forever
o'er the universe must reign.

God of light, shine brightly, even through the gloom of our afflictions. Shine, so that we can see the way to live a righteous life before you. Help us to be gracious, not rude; truthful, not dishonest; patient, not expedient; compassionate, not cruel; full of joy and not despairing. Amen.

Wednesday, April 26 — Psalm 55:1–8
Job 31; 1 Corinthians 7:1–16

There shall once more be heard the voice of mirth and the voice of gladness, the voice of the bridegroom and the voice of the bride, the voices of those who sing, "Give thanks to the Lord of hosts, for the Lord is good, for his steadfast love endures forever!" Jeremiah 33:10-11

The watchers on the mountain 256
proclaim the bridegroom near;
go forth as he approaches
with alleluias clear.
The marriage feast is waiting;
the gates wide open stand.
Arise, O heirs of glory;
the bridegroom is at hand.

The grace of God has appeared, bringing salvation to all. Titus 2:11

Lord Jesus, you are worthy 774*
for all on earth to praise;
our hymns in glad thanksgiving
in gratitude we raise,
for all you did on Calv'ry
when suff'ring on the tree—
the world from sin's dominion
most wondrously set free.

Steadfastly, without fail, you care for us in every time and place, through every joy, change, and hardship. Steadfastly, without consideration of class, race, nation, or species, you offer your love to every living creature. Faithful, steadfast God, how can we keep from singing our thanks and praise? Amen.

Thursday, April 27 — Psalm 55:9–15
Job 32,33; 1 Corinthians 7:17–24

I formed you, you are my servant; O Israel, you will not be forgotten by me. Isaiah 44:21

Abr'ham's seed and Sarah's offspring, *
I have called you forth as mine.
I have brought you into freedom,
giv'n my law to make you kind.
Even when you cry in exile,
I remember your dear name.
I invite, "Come home with gladness,
always in my heart remain."

Has God rejected his people? By no means! Romans 11:1

You are still my chosen people, *
as the many stars above.
You have found in me protection,
freedom, mercy, justice, love.
Never shall I cease to seek you,
never will I you misplace.
You are mine, my cov'nant people,
light for all the human race.

Lord, you extend love and mercy, and call and purpose to Israel—your ancient covenant people—and to all those who inherit your history of leading and guiding them. We give thanks that we, and every other human family, are never beyond the reach of your patient, persistent love. Amen.

Friday, April 28 — Psalm 55:16–19
Job 34:1–28; 1 Corinthians 7:25–40

One who puts on armor should not brag like one who takes it off. 1 Kings 20:11

Lead on, O King eternal, 753
till sin's fierce war shall cease,
and holiness shall whisper
the sweet amen of peace;
for not with sword's loud clashing,
nor roll of stirring drums,
but deeds of love and mercy,
the heav'nly kingdom comes.

Be renewed in the spirit of your minds. Ephesians 4:23

Create in me a clean heart, O God, p79
and renew a right Spirit within me.
Cast me not away from your presence,
and take not your Holy Spirit from me.
Restore unto me the joy of salvation;
anoint me with your Spirit free.
Create in me a clean heart, O God,
and renew a right spirit within me.

We trust you, Lord, to lead us safely through our battles with evil and despair. Before each battle, we beg you to renew our minds with hope, purpose, and peace. We shall not brag until each battle is won, Lord. And then, victorious, we will brag only of you. Amen.

Saturday, April 29 — Psalm 55:20–23
Job 34:29–35:16; 1 Corinthians 8

You shall worship before the Lord your God; and you shall rejoice in every good thing which the Lord your God has given to you and your house. Deuteronomy 26:10-11 ESV

Praise, my soul, the King of heaven, 529
to his feet your tribute bring.
Ransomed, healed, restored, forgiven,
evermore his praises sing.
Alleluia! Alleluia!
Praise the everlasting King!

As for those who in the present age are rich, command them not to be haughty, or to set their hopes on the uncertainty of riches, but rather on God who richly provides us with everything for our enjoyment. They are to do good, to be rich in good works, generous, and ready to share. 1 Timothy 6:17-18

Treasure too you have entrusted, 652*
gain through pow'rs your grace conferred,
ours to use for home and kindred,
and to spread the gospel word.
Open wide our hands in sharing,
as we heed Christ's ageless call,
healing, teaching, and reclaiming,
serving you by loving all.

Every gift comes from you, Lord. May your blessings of wealth and security lead us not to arrogant pride but to humble gratitude. May our gratitude for your gifts lead us not to clutch them tightly, but to open our hands and freely share them with love. Amen.

Fourth Sunday of Easter

Watchword for the week — Jesus said, "I am the gate. Whoever enters by me will be saved, and will come in and go out and find pasture." John 10:9

Sunday, April 30 — Acts 2:42-47; Psalm 23
1 Peter 2:19-25; John 10:1-10

Then Jacob woke from his sleep and said, "Surely the Lord is in this place—and I did not know it!" Genesis 28:16

Let holy thoughts be ours 575
when sleep o'ertakes us;
our earliest thoughts be yours when morning wakes us;
for your dear presence will not leave those lonely
who seek you only.

The disciples said to each other, "Were not our hearts burning within us while he was talking to us on the road, while he was opening the scriptures to us?" Luke 24:32

The path we take, it circles round; *
we seem to come back where it starts;
then you return in bread and word,
and in the yearning of our hearts.
Show us in the breaking of the bread
how to follow, what to say and do.
Claim us with the burning in our hearts.
Tell us who we are to you.

Let us savor, mysterious Lord, those sure moments when we clearly feel you comforting us, hear you calling us, feel you leading us. And then, in moments when you seem just beyond our reach, open our hearts. Let them burn with the power of your ever-present love. Amen.

Monday, May 1 — Psalm 56:1–8
Job 36:1–26; 1 Corinthians 9:1–12a

How great are God's signs, how mighty his wonders! His kingdom is an eternal kingdom; his dominion endures from generation to generation. Daniel 4:3 NIV

Lord, you have been our dwelling place p147
in ev'ry generation.
Your people still have known your grace
and your blessed consolation.
Through ev'ry age you heard our cry,
through ev'ry age we found you nigh,
our strength and our salvation.

Therefore, since we are receiving a kingdom that cannot be shaken, let us give thanks, by which we offer to God an acceptable worship with reverence and awe. Hebrews 12:28

Children of the heav'nly King, 789
as you journey, sweetly sing;
sing your Savior's worthy praise,
glorious in his works and ways.

Dear Lord, help us remember that you built your kingdom on a firm, rock-solid, unshakeable foundation. We stand on that foundation, and nothing shakes us off our rock. We live and move and have our being in you, awestruck at how great your faithful love continues throughout all generations into eternal light and life. We praise you for your wonderful creation and love, for you are the everlasting God of all our days. Our souls sing, "How great thou art!" Amen.

Tuesday, May 2 — Psalm 56:9–13
Job 36:27–37:24; 1 Corinthians 9:12b–27

May the Lord, who is good, pardon everyone who sets his heart on seeking God. 2 Chronicles 30:18-19 NIV

Give deep humility; the sense 750
of godly sorrow give,
a strong desiring confidence
to hear your voice and live.

Jesus said, "I have come to call not the righteous but sinners." Mark 2:17

Come, you sinners, poor and needy, 765
weak and wounded, sick and sore,
Jesus, Son of God, will save you,
full of pity, love, and pow'r.

Sometimes, Lord, we doubt that we can truly have healed hearts, restored relationships, and forgiven, fruitful lives. We seek your forgiveness and we offer forgiveness and love to others as you have offered to us, so that our hearts find a real home in you. In Jesus' name, we pray. Amen.

Wednesday, May 3 — Psalm 57:1–6
Job 38; 1 Corinthians 10:1–10

You shall be holy, for I the Lord your God am holy. Leviticus 19:2

Holy, holy, holy! Though the darkness hide thee, 381
though the eye made blind by sin
thy glory may not see,
only thou art holy; there is none beside thee,
perfect in pow'r, in love, and purity.

We, who were the first to set our hope on Christ, might live for the praise of his glory. Ephesians 1:12

My hope is built on nothing less 771
than Jesus' blood and righteousness;
no merit of my own I claim
but wholly lean on Jesus' name.

Lord, when we lose hope, we also lose sight of your holiness and your call for us to be holy, just as you are. Help us be more like you, and to see clearly where we need to allow you to reshape us into your image. Help us live as you would have us, and help us as we walk together in your footsteps. Amen.

Thursday, May 4 — Psalm 57:7–11
Job 39; 1 Corinthians 10:11–22

My tongue will sing of your promise, for all your commandments are right. Psalm 119:172

Upon your precepts and your ways 510
my heart will meditate with awe;
your word shall be my chief delight,
and I will not forget your law.

I am not ashamed of the gospel; it is the power of God for salvation to everyone who has faith. Romans 1:16

The Savior's blood and righteousness 776*
can be the only proper dress
in which I dare approach that place,
where God shall judge our human race.

Help us remember why we are yours, Lord. Help our voices sing your praises and our hearts and ears remember to listen to your commandments. Help us to put into practice the words and commandments we have learned from you, so that we don't convince ourselves and others that we can simply hear or read your words and not obey or submit to you. In Jesus' name, we pray. Amen.

Friday, May 5 — Psalm 58
Job 40; 1 Corinthians 10:23–11:2

I will remove the guilt of this land in a single day. Zechariah 3:9

Pardon for sin and a peace that endureth, 460*
thine own dear presence to cheer and to guide;
strength for today and bright hope for tomorrow,
blessings all mine, with ten thousand beside!

Jesus Christ is the atoning sacrifice for our sins, and not for ours only but also for the sins of the whole world. 1 John 2:2

Hail, O once despised Jesus! 330
Hail, O Galilean King!
You have suffered to release us,
hope, salvation, joy to bring.
Hail, O agonizing Savior,
bearer of our sin and shame;
by your merits we find favor;
life is given through your name.

Lord, when we practice the two greatest commandments you taught us—to love you first as our God and savior, and to love others as we love ourselves—our souls are filled with light. May we keep the fire burning as we fix our eyes on you. Help us be the hands and feet, to offer a drink of water to the thirsty and take care of those who are sick. Give us the strength to be your body in the world. In your name, O Lord, we pray. Amen.

Saturday, May 6 — Psalm 59:1–9
Job 41; 1 Corinthians 11:3–16

In my distress I called upon the Lord; to my God I cried for help. He heard my voice. Psalm 18:6

To the hills I lift my eyes, 729
the everlasting hills.
Streaming forth in fresh supplies,
my soul the Spirit feels;
will he not his help afford?
Help, while yet I ask, is giv'n;
God comes down, the God and Lord
who made both earth and heav'n.

Jesus was in the stern, asleep on the cushion; and they woke him up and said to him, "Teacher, do you not care that we are perishing?" Mark 4:38

Jesus calls us; o'er the tumult 600
of our life's wild, restless sea,
day by day his voice is sounding,
saying, "Christian, follow me."

We waited for you, Lord, and you heard our cries for help. Even though we think we can trust our survival skills, storms unexpectedly arise that make us realize we could drown without your help. You remain calmly sleeping, reminding us to trust and rest in you until the storm passes, because your love is our protection from what harms us. In your name, Jesus, we thank you for your protection! Amen.

Fifth Sunday of Easter

Watchword for the week — Jesus said, "I am the way, and the truth, and the life. No one comes to the Father except through me." John 14:6

Sunday, May 7 — Acts 7:55-60; Psalm 31:1-5,15-16
1 Peter 2:2-10; John 14:1-14

If your enemies are hungry, give them bread to eat; and if they are thirsty, give them water to drink; for you will heap coals of fire on their heads, and the Lord will reward you. Proverbs 25:21-22

Much forgiven, may I learn 779
love for hatred to return;
then my heart assured shall be
you, my God, have pardoned me.

Love your enemies, do good, and lend, expecting nothing in return. Your reward will be great, and you will be children of the Most High; for he is kind to the ungrateful and the wicked. Luke 6:35

Lest the gifts we offer, 651*
money, talents, time,
serve to salve our conscience,
to our secret shame:
Lord, reprove, inspire us
by the way you give;
teach us, dying Savior,
how true Christians live.

Father, we sometimes hold a grudge and use our words to be spiteful or mean, so that others can feel the pain we are experiencing. Lord, help us let go of the pain and extend kindness and love to all, even to those who are our enemies. You alone are the one who can judge us and take away our sins. Forgive us and forgive our enemies. We thank you for your grace, through our redeemer, Jesus. Amen.

Monday, May 8 — Psalm 59:10–17
Job 42; 1 Corinthians 11:17–30

God said to Moses, "I am who I am." Exodus 3:14

The God of Abraham praise, 468
who reigns enthroned above,
the Ancient of eternal days,
the God of love!
The Lord, the great I Am,
by earth and heav'n confessed—
we bow before his holy name
forever blessed.

If God is for us, who is against us? Romans 8:31

Good Christian friends, rejoice, 291
with heart, and soul, and voice;
now ye need not fear the grave:
Jesus Christ was born to save!
Calls you one and calls you all
to gain his everlasting hall.
Christ was born to save!
Christ was born to save!

O, Lord, we have no reason to be afraid. You bring us life and peace, even when we can't see you and wonder why you are hiding. You are the eternal and great I AM, who has always existed. We have a place at your table, and know that you have plans for our future. In Jesus' name, we pray. Amen!

Tuesday, May 9 — Psalm 60
Proverbs 1:1–2:8; 1 Corinthians 11:31–12:11

The God of heaven will set up a kingdom that shall never be destroyed. Daniel 2:44

The King shall come when morning dawns 257
and light triumphant breaks,
when beauty gilds the eastern hills
and life to joy awakes.

Jesus said to the apostles, "I confer on you, just as my Father has conferred on me, a kingdom, so that you may eat and drink at my table in my kingdom." Luke 22:29-30

Be known to us in breaking bread, 411
but do not then depart;
Savior, abide with us, and spread
your table in our heart.

Jesus, you are our bread of life! Thank you for promising to feed us and care for us always. You know our hunger and thirst for food, for water, and most importantly, your presence in our hearts and lives. Amen and alleluia!

Wednesday, May 10 — Psalm 61
Proverbs 2:9–3:20; 1 Corinthians 12:12–26

Is my hand shortened, that it cannot redeem? Or have I no power to deliver? Isaiah 50:2

"Fear not, I am with you; O be not dismayed, 709
for I am your God and will still give you aid;
I'll strengthen you, help you and cause you to stand
upheld by my righteous, omnipotent hand."

There was a leper who came to Jesus and knelt before him, saying, "Lord, if you choose, you can make me clean." Matthew 8:2

Just as I am; thou wilt receive, 762
wilt welcome, pardon, cleanse, relieve;
because thy promise I believe,
O Lamb of God, I come, I come!

Give us clean hands and a pure heart, Lord, so we can raise them to you. May we give thanks to you, our greatest treasure and most important friend. You are the most high and we praise you! Amen.

Thursday, May 11 — Psalm 62
Proverbs 3:21–4:27; 1 Corinthians 12:27–13:7

Thus says the Lord, "As the wine is found in the cluster, and they say, 'Do not destroy it, for there is a blessing in it', so I will do for my servants' sake, and not destroy them all." Isaiah 65:8

Be present with your servants, Lord; 734
we look to you with one accord;
refresh and strengthen us anew,
and bless what in your name we do.

Indeed, God did not send the Son into the world to condemn the world, but in order that the world might be saved through him. John 3:17

Ye servants of God, your Master proclaim, 565
and publish abroad his wonderful name;
the name all-victorious of Jesus extol;
his kingdom is glorious, he rules over all.

Sometimes our guilt shames us. But you, Lord, come to save us from everything that condemns us and condemns others, including our own negative thoughts. Help us remember to live in freedom because you freed us. Amen.

Friday, May 12 — Psalm 63
Proverbs 5; 1 Corinthians 13:8–14:5

With weeping they shall come, and with consolations I will lead them back, I will let them walk by brooks of water, in a straight path in which they shall not stumble; for I have become a father to Israel. Jeremiah 31:9

My soul he doth restore again, 720
and me to walk doth make
within the paths of righteousness,
e'en for his own name's sake;
within the paths of righteousness,
e'en for his own name's sake.

Jesus said, "You now have sorrow; but I will see you again and your heart will rejoice, and your joy no one will take from you." John 16:22 NKJV

When peace, like a river, attendeth my way, 754
when sorrows like sea billows roll;
whatever my lot, you have taught me to say,
it is well, it is well with my soul.

Jesus, your perfect love casts out our fears. We will walk in your ways because we know our souls are at peace in you. You hear us when we pray for your guidance. Help us make good decisions. In your name, we pray. Amen.

Saturday, May 13 — Psalm 64
Proverbs 6; 1 Corinthians 14:6–19

I am with you to save you and deliver you, says the Lord. Jeremiah 15:20

Your bountiful care what tongue can recite? 566
It breathes in the air; it shines in the light;
it streams from the hills; it descends to the plain,
and sweetly distills in the dew and the rain.

Let us therefore approach the throne of grace with boldness, so that we may receive mercy and find grace to help in time of need. Hebrews 4:16

We come to you, our Father, 433
with thoughts of thanks and praise,
for your abundant mercy,
and all your love and grace;
we praise you for your goodness
and for your loving care,
for daily show'rs of blessing,
for answers to our prayers.

Lord, we have nothing to be afraid of. We are confident that your grace and mercy bring us blessings and joy in times of hardships and sorrow. You wipe away our tears and help us remember that we can come to you in trust, love, and praise for who you are and what you have done for us as our creator, redeemer, and sustainer. Amen!

Sixth Sunday of Easter

Watchword for the week — Make a joyful noise to God, all the earth; sing the glory of his name; give to him glorious praise. Psalm 66:1,2

Sunday, May 14 — Acts 17:22-31; Psalm 66:8-20
1 Peter 3:13-22; John 14:15-21

Daniel said, "My God sent his angel and shut the lions' mouths so that they would not hurt me." Daniel 6:22

Through the long night watches, 567
may your angels spread
their bright wings above me,
watching round my bed.

Jesus said, "My sheep hear my voice. I know them, and they follow me. No one will snatch them out of my hand." John 10:27,28

Jesus makes my heart rejoice, 662
I'm his sheep and know his voice;
he's a Shepherd, kind and gracious,
and his pastures are delicious;
constant love to me he shows,
yea, my very name he knows.

Thank you, Lord, for protecting us when we are attacked by our enemies. We hear your voice, Lord, and follow you to eat in green pastures and drink beside still waters. You are good and kind, the Lion of Judah, and nothing can hurt us because you are our defender. May it be that peace fills our lives and overflows to others around us. Amen.

Monday, May 15 — Psalm 65:1–8
Proverbs 7; 1 Corinthians 14:20–35

Those he gathered from the east and from the west, from the north and from the south: Let them thank the Lord for his steadfast love, for his wonderful works to humankind. Psalm 107:3,8

For the joy of human love, 538
brother, sister, parent, child,
friends on earth, and friends above,
pleasures pure and undefiled,
Lord of all, to you we raise
this our hymn of grateful praise.

Many will come from east and west and will eat with Abraham and Isaac and Jacob in the kingdom of heaven. Matthew 8:11

In Christ there is no east or west, 523
in him no south or north,
but one great fellowship of love
throughout the whole wide earth.

Lord, take the blinders off our eyes. Help us be more accepting of people all over this world. Lord, help us to love others and to be a good friend to them because of your love for us. Help us share your goodness and blessings with everyone. In your name, we pray. Amen!

Tuesday, May 16 — Psalm 65:9–13
Proverbs 8:1–9:6; 1 Corinthians 14:36–15:2

Some sat in darkness and in gloom, prisoners in misery and in irons. Then they cried to the Lord in their trouble, and he saved them from their distress. Let them thank the Lord for his steadfast love, for his wonderful works to humankind. Psalm 107:10,13,15

Since we, though unworthy, 746
through electing grace,
'mid your ransomed people
have obtained a place,
Lord, may we be faithful
to our cov'nant found,
to you, as our shepherd,
and your flock fast bound.

Blessed are those who are persecuted for righteousness' sake, for theirs is the kingdom of heaven. Matthew 5:10

"The soul that on Jesus still leans for repose, 709
I will not, I will not desert to its foes;
that soul, though all hell should endeavor to shake,
I'll never, no, never, no, never forsake!"

Sometimes, Lord, we forget that you are the light in the darkest nights of our souls. Sometimes, real persecution happens to people who are tortured, imprisoned, and martyred for their faith, hope, and trust in you as their guiding light. Help us to recognize the risks involved in being a Christian, and to truly be willing to sacrifice our time and energy for your cause. In the name of the one who died for us, help us live for you. Amen.

Wednesday, May 17 — Psalm 66:1–7
Proverbs 9:7–10:32; 1 Corinthians 15:3–16

O Lord, do not rebuke me in your anger, or discipline me in your wrath. Psalm 6:1

Dear Lord and Father of mankind, 739
forgive our foolish ways;
reclothe us in our rightful mind;
in purer lives thy service find,
in deeper rev'rence, praise.

God has destined us not for wrath but for obtaining salvation through our Lord Jesus Christ, who died for us. 1 Thessalonians 5:9-10

Grounded on your Savior's merit, 515
blessed in his communion sweet,
destined heaven to inherit,
and the church above to meet.

Lord, remind us that the gift of your salvation is free and available to everyone…and that no good works will change that. May we remember the cross and all that you do for us. In your holy name, we pray. Amen.

Ascension Day

Watchword for Ascension Day — Christ said, "I, when I am lifted up from the earth, will draw all people to myself." John 12:32

Ascension of the Lord — Acts 1:1-11; Psalm 47
Ephesians 1:15-23; Luke 24:44-53

Thursday, May 18 — Psalm 66:8–15
Proverbs 11; 1 Corinthians 15:17–28

The human mind may devise many plans, but it is the purpose of the Lord that will be established. Proverbs 19:21

Take my life that it may be 610
all you purpose, Lord, for me.
Take my moments and my days;
let them sing your ceaseless praise,
let them sing your ceaseless praise.

So when they had come together, they asked Jesus, "Lord, is this the time when you will restore the kingdom to Israel?" He replied, "It is not for you to know the times or periods that the Father has set by his own authority. But you will receive power when the Holy Spirit has come upon you; and you will be my witnesses in Jerusalem, in all Judea and Samaria, and to the ends of the earth." Acts 1:6-8

Church, rejoice! Raise your voice, 631
sing Jehovah's worthy praise;
extol his name forever;
laud him, our God and Savior;
proclaim to ev'ry nation
the tidings of salvation;
bear the witness to his greatness;
spread the story of his glory
to the earth's remotest bounds.

Savior, as your disciples witnessed your ascension into heaven, help us to witness your power over all areas of our lives. You came once as a tiny baby, but you will return to earth as a conquering king. We wait with expectation and hope for that glorious day. In your name, we pray. Amen!

Friday, May 19 — Psalm 66:16–20
Proverbs 12; 1 Corinthians 15:29–41

This assembly may know that the Lord does not save by sword and spear. 1 Samuel 17:47

We've a story to tell to the nations, 621
that shall turn their hearts to the right,
a story of truth and mercy,
a story of peace and light,
a story of peace and light.

Jesus said, "Whatever house you enter, first say, 'Peace to this house!'" Luke 10:5

Lord, bless our homes with peace 671*
and love and laughter,
with understanding and with loyalty.
May we together follow Christ the Master
and know the blessing of his sov'reignty.

We ask for peace, Lord, inside our hearts, homes, and families, and outside in our communities and the world around us. We ask you to help us bring peace with open hands and hearts without the need for weapons. Replace our swords with baskets of good gifts from heaven to share with others. Lord Jesus, we ask this in your name. Amen.

* Used by permission of Pilgrim Press/United Church Press.

Saturday, May 20 — Psalm 67
Proverbs 13; 1 Corinthians 15:42–58

I was ready to be sought out by those who did not ask, to be found by those who did not seek me. Isaiah 65:1

Now in the days of youth 801*
when life is filled with choice,
when hope and doubt touch ev'ry hour,
when all thoughts find a voice.
We turn, O God, to you
for guidance and for grace.
In all our days, in all our ways,
help us to seek your face.

But many who are first will be last, and the last will be first. Matthew 19:30

Forbid it, Lord, that I should boast, 350
save in the death of Christ, my God;
all the vain things that charm me most,
I sacrifice them to his blood.

Lord, sometimes we are tempted to put ourselves first before all else, including you and others whom we should love as you love us. Help us remember that the Christian life isn't about us. Help us to love you because you loved us first. Help us show the same love and forgiveness to others and to ourselves. In Jesus name, we pray. Amen.

Ascension Sunday

Watchword for the week — Cast all your anxiety on him, because he cares for you. 1 Peter 5:7

Sunday, May 21 — Acts 1:6-14; Psalm 68:1-10,32-35
1 Peter 4:12-14;5:6-11; John 17:1-11

Restore to me the joy of your salvation, and sustain in me a willing spirit. Psalm 51:12

Come, thou Fount of ev'ry blessing, 782
tune my heart to sing thy grace;
streams of mercy, never ceasing,
call for songs of loudest praise.
Teach me some melodious sonnet,
sung by flaming tongues above.
Praise the mount—I'm fixed upon it—
mount of God's redeeming love.

Are any among you suffering? They should pray. Are any cheerful? They should sing songs of praise. James 5:13

When I tread the verge of Jordan, 790
bid my anxious fears subside;
death of death and hell's destruction,
land me safe on Canaan's side.
Songs and praises, songs and praises,
I will sing forevermore;
I will sing forevermore.

Pain and suffering are hard for us to handle alone, Lord. We need you and our fellow Christians to help carry the load. In good times and in bad, we will remember your presence and give you the offering of our praise. We find joy in your salvation and cheerfully give you—our creator, redeemer, and sustainer—our thanks and praise for blessings and mercy. Amen.

Monday, May 22 — Psalm 68:1–6
Proverbs 14; 1 Corinthians 16:1–11

So I commend enjoyment, for there is nothing better for people under the sun than to eat, and drink, and enjoy themselves, for this will go with them in their toil through the days of life that God gives them under the sun. Ecclesiastes 8:15

My God will lead me to a spot 794
where, all my cares and griefs forgot,
I shall enjoy sweet rest.
As pants for cooling streams the hart,
I languish for my heavenly part,
for God, for God, my Refuge blessed.

Rejoice in the Lord always. Philippians 4:4

Rejoice, the Lord is King! 372
Your Lord and King adore.
Rejoice, give thanks and sing
and triumph evermore.
Lift up your heart, lift up your voice,
rejoice, again I say, rejoice!

Creating God, help our voices praise you. Redeeming God, help us find the balance between work and rest. Sustaining God, bring joy to our hearts for every moment of our lives. Journeying God, help us walk with others, so that we can share what you have given us, and remember how you have been faithful in caring for all. Amen.

Tuesday, May 23 — Psalm 68:7–18
Proverbs 15; 1 Corinthians 16:12–24

You must therefore be careful to do as the Lord your God has commanded you; you shall not turn to the right or to the left. Deuteronomy 5:32

So may I prove true, 608
devoted to you,
and cheerfully stand,
prepared to comply with your ev'ry command.

Jesus said to him, "'You shall love the Lord your God with all your heart, and with all your soul, and with all your mind.' This is the greatest and first commandment. And a second is like it: 'You shall love your neighbor as yourself.'" Matthew 22:37-39

Christian hearts, in love united, 673
seek alone in Jesus rest;
has he not your love excited?
Then let love inspire each breast.
Members—on our Head depending,
lights—reflecting him, our Sun,
brethren—his commands attending,
we in him, our Lord, are one.

God of love, help us remember to be love in action and in thought. Help us to depend upon you, and be willing to put into action what you have asked us to do. Help us feed hungry people; help us mend broken hearts. Help us be the mirror that other people look into to see your reflection. In your redeeming name, we pray. Amen.

Wednesday, May 24 — Psalm 68:19–27
Proverbs 16; 2 Corinthians 1:1–11

When my spirit grows faint within me, it is you who watch over my way. Psalm 142:3 NIV

In heav'nly love abiding, 732
no change my heart shall fear;
and safe is such confiding,
for nothing changes here.
The storm may roar around me,
my heart may low be laid,
but God is round about me,
and can I be dismayed?

Come to me, all you that are weary and are carrying heavy burdens, and I will give you rest. Matthew 11:28

Are we weak and heavy laden, 743
cumbered with a load of care?
Precious Savior, still our refuge,
take it to the Lord in prayer!
Do your friends despise, forsake you?
Take it to the Lord in prayer!
In his arms he'll take and shield you;
you will find a solace there.

Lord, you are more than a security blanket. You are a watchtower and a resting place in our lives. We have nothing to fear, because you take care of us. Amen!

Thursday, May 25 — Psalm 68:28–35
Proverbs 17; 2 Corinthians 1:12–22

But you, O Bethlehem of Ephrathah, who are one of the little clans of Judah, from you shall come forth for me one who is to rule in Israel, whose origin is from of old, from ancient days. Micah 5:2

O little town of Bethlehem, 282
how still we see thee lie;
above thy deep and dreamless sleep
the silent stars go by.
Yet in thy dark streets shineth
the everlasting light;
the hopes and fears of all the years
are met in thee tonight.

Without any doubt, the mystery of our religion is great: He was revealed in flesh, vindicated in spirit, seen by angels, proclaimed among Gentiles, believed in throughout the world, taken up in glory. 1 Timothy 3:16

Church, go forth o'er the earth; 631
Christ, your head, has hallowed you,
a chosen bride forever,
adorned now for our Savior;
be strong and be not cheerless,
and may your saints be fearless;
in all places, with all races,
may that story of his glory
be the hope of all the world.

Lord, sometimes we forget that Christmas, Good Friday, Easter, and Ascension Day are all parts of one story, but the story doesn't end there. Your birth, life, death, burial, resurrection, and ascension are important because they happened for our salvation. We believe you are coming back for us and for the whole church. We thank you for that hope! Amen.

Friday, May 26 — Psalm 69:1–12
Proverbs 18; 2 Corinthians 1:23–2:13

The Lord our God is righteous in everything he does. Daniel 9:14 NIV

His righteous government and power 320
shall over all extend;
on judgment and on justice based,
his reign shall have no end.

God [did] prove at the present time that he himself is righteous and that he justifies the one who has faith in Jesus. Romans 3:25-26

When he shall come with trumpet sound, 771
O may I then in him be found
clothed in his righteousness alone,
redeemed to stand before the throne.

Lord, there is nothing we can do to earn our salvation except to ask you to help our hearts believe in you and to put your teachings into practice. Thank you for giving us your hope, righteousness, and salvation. Amen!

Saturday, May 27 — Psalm 69:13–21
Proverbs 19; 2 Corinthians 2:14–3:11

A faithful God, without deceit, just and upright is he. Deuteronomy 32:4

Great is thy faithfulness, O God my Father, 460*
there is no shadow of turning with thee;
thou changest not, thy compassions they fail not;
as thou hast been thou forever wilt be.

And by this we know that he abides in us, by the Spirit that he has given us. 1 John 3:24

Join we all with one accord; 525
praise we all our common Lord;
for we all have heard his voice,
all have made his will our choice.
Join we with the saints of old,
no more strangers in the fold,
one the Shepherd who us sought,
one the flock his blood has bought.

Thank you, Lord, for giving us your Spirit when you chose us to be your children. We praise you for bringing us into your family with common goals of preaching the gospel and bringing hope to the world. We thank you for the variety of gifts you give us to help work towards that goal. Thank you for the ongoing work of redemption and transformation into your image, through the Holy Spirit. We thank you for your unconditional love that never changes nor is hidden from us. Amen!

Day of Pentecost

Watchword for the week — Now there are varieties of gifts, but the same Spirit; and there are varieties of services, but the same Lord. 1 Corinthians 12:4,5

Sunday, May 28 — Acts 2:1-21; Psalm 104:24-34,35b
1 Corinthians 12:3b-13; John 20:19-23

For I will be a wall of fire around [Jerusalem], says the Lord. Zechariah 2:5

Glorious things of you are spoken, 522
Zion, city of our God;
he whose word cannot be broken
formed you for his own abode;
on the rock of ages founded,
what can shake your sure repose?
With salvation's walls surrounded
you may smile at all your foes.

When the day of Pentecost had come, divided tongues, as of fire, appeared among them, and a tongue rested on each of them. All of them were filled with the Holy Spirit. Acts 2:1,3-4

Like divided tongues of flame 375*
on the twelve the Spirit came—
tongues, that earth may hear their call,
fire, that love may burn in all.
Alleluia!

Thank you for protecting us and keeping us safe, Lord. Help us spread the good news of great joy like a holy fire that lights our way and keeps us warm. Help us bring hope and light to the world around us in ways that people can understand for themselves. Fill us with your Spirit and enable us to offer protection and peace to others who need it. In your name, we pray. Amen.

Monday, May 29 — Psalm 69:22–29
Proverbs 20; 2 Corinthians 3:12–4:6

"The silver is mine, and the gold is mine," says the Lord of hosts. Haggai 2:8

As you, Lord, have lived for others, 648
so may we for others live;
freely have your gifts been granted;
freely may your servants give.
Yours the gold and yours the silver,
yours the wealth of land and sea;
we but stewards of your bounty
held in solemn trust will be.

Now the whole group of those who believed were of one heart and soul, and no one claimed private ownership of any possessions, but everything they owned was held in common. Acts 4:32

Take my wealth, all I possess, 647
make me rich in faithfulness.
Take my mind that I may use
ev'ry pow'r as you should choose.

All that we have is really from you, Lord. Help us offer the first fruits of everything to you. We intentionally choose to be selfless and cheerful givers instead of selfish and cheerless hoarders of what we think we should have to live an abundant life. Help us and our fellow Christians meet the needs of the communities we live in. In Jesus' name, we pray. Amen.

Tuesday, May 30 — Psalm 69:30–36
Proverbs 21; 2 Corinthians 4:7–18

Is the Lord's arm too short? Numbers 11:23 NIV

Under the shadow of your throne 461
your saints have dwelt secure;
sufficient is your arm alone,
and our defense is sure.

Jesus said, "Again, truly I tell you, if two of you agree on earth about anything you ask, it will be done for you by my Father in heaven." Matthew 18:19

'Tis a pleasant thing to see 670
brothers in the Lord agree,
sisters of a God of love
live as they shall live above,
acting each a Christian part,
one in word and one in heart.

Sometimes we stumble and fall, Lord. Sometimes, we don't forgive others the way you forgive us. But when you reach out to rescue us with a long, outstretched arm, it helps us to open our arms to those who need your forgiveness. Help us to be forgiving of each other and to live in peace and agreement with your plans for our lives. In awe of your name, we pray. Amen.

Wednesday, May 31 — Psalm 70
Proverbs 22; 2 Corinthians 5:1–15

You have turned my mourning into dancing; you have taken off my sackcloth and clothed me with joy. Psalm 30:11

Ten thousand times ten thousand 394
in sparkling raiment bright,
the armies of the ransomed saints
throng up the steeps of light!
'Tis finished, all is finished,
their fight with death and sin.
Fling open wide the golden gates
and let the victors in!

May the God of hope fill you with all joy and peace in believing, so that you may abound in hope by the power of the Holy Spirit. Romans 15:13

Lord of all hopefulness, Lord of all joy, 802*
whose trust, ever childlike no cares could destroy:
be there at our waking, and give us, we pray,
your bliss in our hearts, Lord, at the break of the day.

Sustaining and comforting Spirit, you fill us with joy, even when we mourn and grieve for losses we have faced. You replace the broken and shredded parts of our lives with complete and sturdy walls to support us through challenges. Your light is a beacon of hope for us to find our way back to you. Thank you for redeeming love that keeps us warm. Amen!

Thursday, June 1 — Psalm 71:1–8
Proverbs 23; 2 Corinthians 5:16–6:2

He will swallow up death forever. Isaiah 25:8

It was a strange and dreadful strife 367
when life and death contended;
the victory remained with life:
the reign of death was ended.
Stripped of pow'r, no more it reigns,
an empty form alone remains;
death's sting is lost forever!
Alleluia!

I want to know Christ and the power of his resurrection and the sharing of his sufferings by becoming like him in his death, if somehow I may attain the resurrection from the dead. Philippians 3:10-11

You are the life; the rending tomb 661
proclaims your conqu'ring arm;
and those who put their trust in you
not death nor hell shall harm.

Dear God, may we partake of all the sufferings in our lives in humble obedience to you, and may we be increasingly transformed into the image of Jesus Christ, our Lord, in whose name we pray. Amen.

Friday, June 2 — Psalm 71:9–18a
Proverbs 24; 2 Corinthians 6:3–18

"In this place I will give peace," says the Lord of hosts. Haggai 2:9 NKJV

Lord, be near us here 542*
our sad lives to cheer;
stand beside us, ever guide us,
Lord, be near us here.

And let the peace of Christ rule in your hearts, to which indeed you were called in the one body. And be thankful. Colossians 3:15

In Christ shall true hearts ev'rywhere 523
their high communion find;
his service is the golden cord
close binding humankind.

Greatest Lord, you call us into community and bind us together as the body of Christ. Strengthen us to seek peace with one another and to act in love. Help us to not lose sight of your goodness. Accept our humble gratitude for all you give to us, for you have given us all. Amen.

* Albert H. Frank.

Saturday, June 3 — Psalm 71:18b–24
Proverbs 25; 2 Corinthians 7:1–13a

Behold, your King is coming to you; He is just and having salvation, lowly and riding on a donkey. Zechariah 9:9 NKJV

Prepare the royal highway; 344*
the King of kings is near!
Let ev'ry hill and valley
a level road appear!
Then greet the king of glory
foretold in sacred story.

Jesus said, "Blessed are the meek, for they will inherit the earth." Matthew 5:5

Take my hands, Lord Jesus, 578**
let them work for you,
make them strong and gentle, kind in all I do;
let me watch you, Jesus, till I'm gentle too,
till my hands are kind hands, quick to work for you.

Most Holy Lord our God, we confess that our desire for power and possessions separates us from you. We long for more, even as your son came riding on a donkey. Forgive us, we pray, and give us the faith to follow Jesus' example of gentleness and strength for the sake of others. Amen.

Trinity Sunday

Watchword for the week — O Lord, our Sovereign, how majestic is your name in all the earth! Psalm 8:9

Sunday, June 4 — Genesis 1:1-2:4a; Psalm 8
2 Corinthians 13:11-13; Matthew 28:16-20

The Lord is just in all his ways, and kind in all his doings. Psalm 145:17

O bless the Lord, my soul! 546
His mercies bear in mind!
Forget not all his benefits!
The Lord to all is kind.

I am confident of this, that the one who began a good work among you will bring it to completion by the day of Jesus Christ. Philippians 1:6

Finish, then, your new creation; 474
pure and spotless let us be;
let us see your great salvation
perfectly restored and free.
Changed from glory into glory,
till in heav'n we take our place,
till we cast our crowns before you,
lost in wonder, love, and praise.

You are God the creator, from whom all blessings flow. You are Christ the savior of the world, by whose blood we are set free. You are the Spirit of truth and love, through whom we can fulfill your calling for our lives. Eternal Trinity, we praise and adore you forever. Amen.

Monday, June 5 — Psalm 72:1–11
Proverbs 26; 2 Corinthians 7:13b–8:9

Fathers make known to children your faithfulness. Isaiah 38:19

All this for us your love has done; p54
by this to you our love is won;
for this we sing through all our days
and shout our thanks in ceaseless praise.

As you therefore have received Christ Jesus the Lord, continue to live your lives in him, rooted and built up in him and established in the faith, just as you were taught, abounding in thanksgiving. Colossians 2:6-7

Let all who have received Christ 434*
now live life in the Lord
abounding in thanksgiving
for God's affirming word.
To us are given glad hearts
as we reflect Love's grace.
We know who we are called to be.
Now claiming our identity
as God's own people let us be
a living alleluia!

Loving God, we have received all we need to live a life worthy of Christ Jesus. Help us, we pray, to center our lives on him and to reflect his love in who we are and all we do. Amen.

Tuesday, June 6 — Psalm 72:12–20
Proverbs 27; 2 Corinthians 8:10–21

Out of the ground the Lord God formed every animal of the field and every bird of the air, and brought them to the man. The man gave names to [all]. Genesis 2:19,20

This is our Father's world: 456
O let us not forget
that though the wrong is often strong,
God is the ruler yet.
He trusts us with his world,
to keep it clean and fair—
all earth and trees, all skies and seas,
all creatures ev'rywhere.

Are not five sparrows sold for two pennies? Yet not one of them is forgotten in God's sight. Luke 12:6

Summer and winter, 460*
and springtime and harvest,
sun, moon, and stars in their courses above
join with all nature in manifold witness
to thy great faithfulness, mercy, and love.

Almighty God, how lucky we are to live in your world and to be your beloved children. May we do all within our power to care for your precious creation just as you care so tenderly for us. Amen.

Wednesday, June 7 — Psalm 73:1–12
Proverbs 28; 2 Corinthians 8:22–9:9

You must follow exactly the path that the Lord your God has commanded you, so that you may live. Deuteronomy 5:33

As it was without beginning, 458
so it lasts without an end;
to their children's children ever
shall God's righteousness extend:
unto such as keep God's cov'nant
and are steadfast in his way,
unto those who still remember
the commandments and obey.

For whatever was written in former days was written for our instruction, so that by steadfastness and by the encouragement of the scriptures we might have hope. Romans 15:4

O word of God incarnate, 505
O wisdom from on high,
O truth unchanged, unchanging,
O light of our dark sky:
we praise you for the radiance
that from the scripture's page,
a lantern to our footsteps,
shines on from age to age.

Heavenly Father, you are the way and yet we wander, looking for fulfillment everywhere but through you. Help us to surrender ourselves to you and to listen for your direction. Guide us to your holy word so that we may live the lives you would have us live, always hoping in Christ Jesus, our Lord, in whose name, we pray. Amen.

Thursday, June 8 — Psalm 73:13–20
Proverbs 29; 2 Corinthians 9:10–10:6

Boaz said to Ruth, "May you have a full reward from the Lord, under whose wings you have come for refuge!" Ruth 2:12

God be with you till we meet again; 824
'neath his wings protecting hide you,
daily manna still provide you:
God be with you till we meet again.

Christ came and proclaimed peace to you who were far off and peace to those who were near. Ephesians 2:17

May the God of hope go with us ev'ry day, 708
filling all our lives with love and joy and peace.
May the God of justice speed us on our way,
bringing light and hope to ev'ry land and race.

You are the author of all that is good, dear Lord, our ever-present source of comfort and strength. Use our lives, we pray, to be instruments of your peace and healing. Amen.

Friday, June 9 — Psalm 73:21–28
Proverbs 30; 2 Corinthians 10:7–18

The Lord your God turned the curse into a blessing for you, because the Lord your God loved you. Deuteronomy 23:5

God forgives all your transgressions, 458
all diseases gently heals,
God redeems you from destruction,
and with you so kindly deals.

Regard the patience of our Lord as salvation. 2 Peter 3:15

Now shall the church, this time of celebration, 830*
give thanks to God for each new revelation,
for gospel truth and promise of salvation:
to God be endless praise!

Glorious God, we thank you for your love, unconditional and eternal. We thank you for salvation, full and free. We thank you for the assurance that nothing can separate us from you. Keep us close, we pray, as we strive to live so that we are worthy to stand before Jesus when he comes. Amen.

Saturday, June 10 — Psalm 74:1–9
Proverbs 31; 2 Corinthians 11:1–11

I will satisfy the weary, and all who are faint I will replenish. Jeremiah 31:25

My Shepherd will supply my need; 730
the Lord God is his name.
In pastures fresh he makes me feed,
beside the living stream.
He brings my wand'ring spirit back
when I forsake his ways,
and leads me for his mercy's sake
in paths of truth and grace.

Jesus said, "Blessed are the poor in spirit, for theirs is the kingdom of heaven." Matthew 5:3

Blessed are the poor in spirit, 595
claiming nothing as their own,
but as giv'n them by their Father
that his goodness may be shown.
Blessed are they who share the sorrow
of their God's unchanging love;
they shall know his presence with them
and his promised comfort prove.

You are the strength of your people, O Lord; your goodness and love made us alive when we were dead. Help us to turn to you when we are worn down. Keep us from pride and give us humble and grateful hearts. Amen.

Second Sunday after Pentecost

Watchword for the week — God desires steadfast love and not sacrifice, the knowledge of God rather than burnt offerings. Hosea 6:6

Sunday, June 11 — Hosea 5:15-6:6; Psalm 50:7-15
Romans 4:13-25; Matthew 9:9-13,18-26

Turn back to the Lord whom you have deeply betrayed. Isaiah 31:6

Out of the depths I cry to you; 761*
O Father, hear me calling.
Incline your ear to my distress
in spite of my rebelling.
Do not regard my sinful deeds.
Send me the grace my spirit needs;
without it I am nothing.

The saying is sure and worthy of full acceptance, that Christ Jesus came into the world to save sinners. 1 Timothy 1:15

Lord Jesus, you are worthy 774**
for all on earth to praise;
our hymns in glad thanksgiving
in gratitude we raise,
for all you did on Calv'ry
when suff'ring on the tree—
the world from sin's dominion
most wondrously set free.

We confess to you, merciful Savior, that our sins are many. Daily we fail to live as your children and to obey your word. Forgive us, we humbly pray, and hear now our shouts of joy for the salvation we receive through Jesus Christ, our Lord. Amen.

Monday, June 12 — Psalm 74:10–17
Ecclesiastes 1:1–3:8; 2 Corinthians 11:12–15

Consider my affliction and my trouble, and forgive all my sins. Psalm 25:18

Lord, forgive me, day by day 779
debts I cannot hope to pay,
duties I have left undone,
evils I have failed to shun.

Just so, I tell you, there will be more joy in heaven over one sinner who repents than over ninety-nine righteous persons who need no repentance. Luke 15:7

Here I find my greatest treasure; 782
hither by thy help I've come;
and I hope, by thy good pleasure,
safely to arrive at home.
Jesus sought me when a stranger,
wand'ring from the fold of God;
he, to rescue me from danger,
bought me with his precious blood.

Redeemer God, we kneel before you burdened and broken. Like David, we are aware of our sins and pray for mercy. Help us to live in the radiance of your forgiveness through Christ, in whose name we pray. Amen.

Tuesday, June 13 — Psalm 74:18–23
Ecclesiastes 3:9–5:20; 2 Corinthians 11:16–33

And now, therefore, let the power of the Lord be great in the way that you promised. Numbers 14:17

What God's almighty pow'r has made, 537
in mercy he is keeping;
by morning glow or evening shade
his eye is never sleeping.
And where he rules in kingly might,
there all is just and all is right:
to God all praise and glory!

Mary said, "The Mighty One has done great things for me, and holy is his name." Luke 1:49

My soul magnifies the Lord, p232
and my spirit rejoices in God my Savior,
for he has looked with favor
  on the lowliness of his servant.
Surely, from now on all generations
  will call me blessed;
for the Mighty One has done great things for me,
and holy is his name.

Heavenly Father, we recognize the wondrous ways you are at work in our lives from the rising of the sun to the place where it sets. With gratitude and awe, we praise your most mighty and holy name. Amen.

Wednesday, June 14 — Psalm 75
Ecclesiastes 6:1–7:14; 2 Corinthians 12:1–13

My soul will boast in the Lord; let the afflicted hear and rejoice. Psalm 34:2 NIV

Praise him for his grace and favor 529
to his people in distress.
Praise him, still the same forever,
slow to chide, and swift to bless.
Alleluia! Alleluia!
Glorious in his faithfulness!

Rejoice. Let your gentleness be known to everyone. The Lord is near. Philippians 4:4,5

Jesus is my joy, 594
therefore blessed am I;
O his mercy is unbounded,
all my hope on him is grounded;
Jesus is my joy,
therefore blessed am I.

With our whole hearts we sing to you, O God, for sending Jesus to show us how to live. May the joy we feel because of his presence be evident in all we do. Amen.

Thursday, June 15 — Psalm 76
Ecclesiastes 7:15–9:18; 2 Corinthians 12:14–13:4

"'I will not hide my face from them anymore; for I shall have poured out my Spirit on the house of Israel,' says the Lord God." Ezekiel 39:29 NKJV

God sends us his Spirit to befriend and help us, 493*
recreate and guide us, Spirit-Friend.
Spirit who enlivens, sanctifies, enlightens,
sets us free, is now our Spirit-Friend.

It is that very Spirit bearing witness with our spirit that we are children of God. Romans 8:16

Now we are God's people, 493*
bonded by his presence,
agents of his purpose, Spirit-Friend.
Lead us forward ever, slipping backward never,
to your remade world, our Spirit-Friend.

Holy Spirit, we thank you for the many ways you mold and transform us, and for your assurance that we are children of God. Bring us ever closer and guide us in the ways in which we should live as God's family. Amen.

Friday, June 16 — Psalm 77:1–9
Ecclesiastes 10:1–12:14; 2 Corinthians 13:5–13

Far be it from us that we should rebel against the Lord, and turn away this day from following the Lord. Joshua 22:29

Lord, obediently we go, 789
gladly leaving all below;
lead us now in all we do
and we still will follow you.

Let us consider not neglecting to meet together, as is the habit of some, but encouraging one another. Hebrews 10:25

Blessed Jesus, at your word 558
we are gathered all to hear you;
let our hearts and souls be stirred
now to seek and love and fear you;
by your teachings true and holy,
drawn from earth to love you solely.

Lord, we confess that we often stray. We follow our own desires. We isolate ourselves. We fail to uplift others. Have mercy on us, O God, and bring us closer to one another as we strive to draw closer to you. Amen.

Saturday, June 17 — Psalm 77:10–15
Song of Solomon 1:1–2:7; Galatians 1:1–12

The mighty one, God the Lord, speaks and summons the earth from the rising of the sun to its setting. Psalm 50:1

Angels help us to adore him, 529
who behold him face to face.
Sun and moon bow down before him;
all who dwell in time and space.
Alleluia! Alleluia!
Praise with us the God of grace.

Jesus said, "The kingdom of God is not coming with things that can be observed; nor will they say, 'Look, here it is!' or 'There it is!' For, in fact, the kingdom of God is among you." Luke 17:20-21

Let us recall that in our midst, 785*
dwells Christ, God's holy Son;
as members of each body joined,
in him we are made one.

You call to us, sovereign God, and we wake to hear you. Open our ears to listen for your voice through Jesus Christ, our Lord, who lives among us, and is our hope now and always. Amen.

Third Sunday after Pentecost

Watchword for the week — The Lord is good; his steadfast love endures forever, and his faithfulness to all generations. Psalm 100:5

Sunday, June 18 — Exodus 19:2-8a; Psalm 100
Romans 5:1-8; Matthew 9:35-10:8,(9-23)

The heavens are yours, the earth also is yours; the world and all that is in it—you have founded them. The north and the south—you created them. Psalm 89:11-12

God is love, let heav'n adore him; 463
God is love, let earth rejoice;
let creation sing before him
and exalt him with one voice.
God who laid the earth's foundation,
God who spread the heav'ns above,
God who breathes through all creation:
God is love, eternal love.

All things have been created through Christ and for him. He himself is before all things, and in him all things hold together. Colossians 1:16-17

You only are the Holy One 472*
who came for our salvation,
and only you are God's true Son
who was before creation.
You only, Christ, as Lord we own,
and with the Spirit you alone
share in the Father's glory.

Creator God, sometimes we forget that all things are made by you, and that we need to care for it as a precious gift. Show us how to honor and care for your world; empower us to act for the good of all. May we follow your lead and love your creation as much as you do. In Jesus' name, we pray. Amen.

Monday, June 19 — Psalm 77:16–20
Song of Solomon 2:8–4:16; Galatians 1:13–24

All who forsake you shall be put to shame; for they have forsaken the fountain of living water, the Lord. Jeremiah 17:13

Lord God, with shame I now confess p32
I've turned away from you;
forgive me all my sins today,
my heart and soul renew.

God said, "To the thirsty I will give water as a gift from the spring of the water of life." Revelation 21:6

I heard the voice of Jesus say, 606
"Behold, I freely give
the living water; thirsty one,
stoop down and drink and live."
I came to Jesus, and I drank
of that life-giving stream;
my thirst was quenched, my soul revived,
and now I live in him.

Holy One, we give you thanks for your saving water of life, a free gift of your grace. Remind us today, Lord, that you alone will quench our thirst, and give us bodies and souls willing to take a drink. Amen.

Tuesday, June 20 — Psalm 78:1–8
Song of Solomon 5,6; Galatians 2:1–14

The Lord will regard the prayer of the destitute, and will not despise their prayer. Psalm 102:17

I fully am persuaded 769
and joyfully declare
I'm never left unaided,
my Father hears my prayer;
his comforts never fail me,
he stands at my right hand;
when tempests fierce assail me,
they're calm at his command.

Do not worry about anything, but in everything by prayer and supplication with thanksgiving let your requests be made known to God. Philippians 4:6

Sing alleluia, Christ does live, 364
and peace on earth restore;
come, ransomed souls, and glory give,
sing, worship and adore:
to him our heartfelt thanks we pay
in deep humility.
It's God alone whose saving way
has set believers free.

Lord, we call on you today. You know what is on our minds and we bring those concerns to you. You hear us and care for us, and we thank you for how you are at work in our lives. We will strive to focus not on our anxieties, but on your presence and peace. Amen.

Wednesday, June 21 — Psalm 78:9–16
Song of Solomon 7,8; Galatians 2:15–3:5

Relieve the troubles of my heart, and bring me out of my distress. Psalm 25:17

Lord, we cry to you for help. 760*
Only you can heal our pain.
Out of deep distress we call.
Help us, Lord; send peace again.

Jesus said, "In this world you will have trouble. But take heart! I have overcome the world." John 16:33 NIV

Peace, perfect peace, our future all unknown? 710
Jesus we know, and he is on the throne.

Lamb of God, we can face anything because your victory is our victory. Thank you that we have nothing to fear with you as our savior. May our hearts rest in you, in whose name we pray. Amen.

Thursday, June 22 — Psalm 78:17–31
Isaiah 1; Galatians 3:6–18

Lord, remember and do not break your covenant with us. Jeremiah 14:21

It is in God that we shall hope, 761*
and not in our own merit.
We rest our fears in his good word
and trust his Holy Spirit.
His promise keeps us strong and sure;
we trust the holy signature
inscribed upon our temples.

God is faithful; by him you were called into the fellowship of his Son, Jesus Christ our Lord. 1 Corinthians 1:9

Come then, come, O flock of Jesus, 673
covenant with him anew;
unto him, who conquered for us,
pledge we love and service true;
and should our love's union holy
firmly linked no more remain,
wait ye at his footstool lowly,
till he draw it close again.

Faithful God, we give thanks that you are the same yesterday, today, and forever. We rejoice that you call us into fellowship with your son, our Lord Jesus Christ, and pray that we may remember who we are in him. Amen.

Friday, June 23 — Psalm 78:32–39
Isaiah 2:1–4:1; Galatians 3:19–29

The Lord said to Moses, "All the people among whom you live shall see the work of the Lord." Exodus 34:10

Holy God, we praise your name: 386
Lord of all, we bow before you.
Saints on earth your rule acclaim;
all in heaven above adore you.
Infinite your vast domain;
everlasting is your reign.

Jesus went throughout Galilee, teaching in their synagogues and proclaiming the good news of the kingdom and curing every disease and every sickness among the people. Matthew 4:23

And then your touch brought life and health, 736*
gave speech, and strength, and sight;
and youth renewed and health restored,
claimed you, the Lord of light:
and so, O Lord, be near to bless,
almighty now as then,
in ev'ry street, in ev'ry home,
in ev'ry troubled friend.

Amazing Lord Jesus, you blessed the world with your teaching, preaching, and healing. May we follow your example and look to ease suffering, offer care, and share the good news wherever we go. In your holy name, we pray. Amen.

Saturday, June 24 — Psalm 78:40–55
Isaiah 4:2–5:30; Galatians 4:1–16

He has told you, O mortal, what is good; and what does the Lord require of you but to do justice, and to love kindness, and to walk humbly with your God? Micah 6:8

What does the Lord require 695*
for praise and offering?
What sacrifice, desire, or tribute bid you bring?
Do justly, love mercy, walk humbly with your God.

Let the same mind be in you that was in Christ Jesus. Philippians 2:5

May the mind of Christ my Savior 585
live in me from day to day,
by his love and pow'r controlling
all I do and say.

What you ask of us is simple, O God, and you have shown us what is good; still, we need your help to do what is required. Give us the strength and compassion to have the same mind as Jesus: showing concern for all people, offering ourselves in service to everyone, and relying totally on you. Amen.

Fourth Sunday after Pentecost

Watchword for the week — Jesus said, "Those who find their life will lose it, and those who lose their life for my sake will find it." Matthew 10:39

Sunday, June 25 — Jeremiah 20:7-13; Psalm 69:7-10,(11-15)16-18 Romans 6:1b-11; Matthew 10:24-39

The revelation awaits an appointed time; though it lingers, wait for it. Habakkuk 2:3 NIV

Keep bright in us the vision 683*
of days when war shall cease,
when hatred and division
give way to love and peace,
till dawns the morning glorious
when truth and justice reign,
and Christ shall rule victorious
o'er all the world's domain.

Therefore be serious and discipline yourselves for the sake of your prayers. Above all, maintain constant love for one another. 1 Peter 4:7-8

And in your love may we abide, 519
estranged from none by wrath or pride,
among ourselves at unity
and with all else in charity.

Everlasting God, as we wait patiently for what lies beyond the trials and struggles of this life, may we do so as the body of Christ, trusting in you and loving one another fully. Amen.

Monday, June 26 — Psalm 78:56–64
Isaiah 6,7; Galatians 4:17–27

Even though I walk through the darkest valley, I fear no evil; for you are with me; your rod and your staff—they comfort me. Psalm 23:4

When I walk through the shades of death, 730
your presence is my stay;
one word of your supporting breath
drives all my fears away.
Your hand, in sight of all my foes,
shall still my table spread;
my cup with blessings overflows;
your oil anoints my head.

We are afflicted in every way, but not crushed; perplexed, but not driven to despair; persecuted, but not forsaken; struck down, but not destroyed. 2 Corinthians 4:8-9

I do not know what may befall 727*
of grief or gladness, peace or pain;
but I know Christ, and through it all
I know his presence will sustain.

Great Shepherd, we give you thanks for walking with us every moment of our lives, and for lifting us from the despairs of this world. May we find true comfort and peace in you, our ever-present Lord and Savior. Amen.

Tuesday, June 27 — Psalm 78:65–72
Isaiah 8:1–9:7; Galatians 4:28–5:6

Then all flesh shall know that I am the Lord your Savior, and your Redeemer. Isaiah 49:26

Before the Lord's eternal throne, 455
you nations, bow with sacred joy;
know that the Lord is God alone;
he can create, and he destroy.

Jesus said, "All authority in heaven and on earth has been given to me. Go therefore and make disciples of all nations, baptizing them in the name of the Father and of the Son and of the Holy Spirit, and teaching them to obey everything that I have commanded you." Matthew 28:18-20

Lord, you call us to your service: 617*
"In my name baptize and teach."
That the world may trust your promise—
life abundant meant for each—
give us all new fervor, draw us
closer in community;
with the Spirit's gifts empow'r us
for the work of ministry.

It is our desire to know you, Savior and Redeemer, and to become your true disciples. Make us willing to learn, we pray, so that we may grow closer to you. Strengthen us for the important work of spreading your gospel, so that all the world may know of your love. Amen.

Wednesday, June 28 — Psalm 79:1–8
Isaiah 9:8–10:11; Galatians 5:7–18

I give thanks to your name for your steadfast love and your faithfulness; for you have exalted your name and your word above everything. Psalm 138:2

Now thank we all our God 533
with heart and hands and voices,
who wondrous things has done,
in whom his world rejoices;
who, from our mother's arms,
has blessed us on our way
with countless gifts of love,
and still is ours today.

You have been born anew, not of perishable but of imperishable seed, through the living and enduring word of God. 1 Peter 1:23

God's word alive and active 503*
our song of songs will be;
its message we will follow
throughout eternity.
And when the saints are gathered
and death has ceased to be,
we'll praise our wondrous Maker
in songs of victory.

We bow before you, O Lord, grateful recipients of your steadfast love and faithfulness. We lift your name above all others, unworthy recipients of a new life in Christ Jesus. We thank you and put all our hope in you, our eternal God, world without end. Amen.

Thursday, June 29 — Psalm 79:9–13
Isaiah 10:12–11:9; Galatians 5:19–6:5

**The Lord is with me as a mighty, awesome One.
Jeremiah 20:11 NKJV**

God reveals his presence; 554
let us now adore him
and with awe appear before him.
God is in his temple;
all in us keep silence
and before him bow with reverence.
Him alone God we own;
he's our Lord and Savior.
Praise his name forever.

**I am grateful to Christ Jesus our Lord, who has strengthened me, because he judged me faithful.
1 Timothy 1:12**

When the Spirit of God is within us, 549*
we will overcome.
In our weakness his strength will defend us,
when his praise is on our tongue.
So lift your voices, with gladness sing;
proclaim through all the earth
that Jesus Christ is King!

We praise your name, O God, our protector and defender, and give you thanks for the gift of your son, Jesus Christ, who leads, strengthens, and redeems us. We offer ourselves to you today, that we may be used for your glory. Amen.

Friday, June 30 — Psalm 80:1–7
Isaiah 11:10–13:22; Galatians 6:6–18

When people fall, do they not get up again? If they go astray, do they not turn back? Jeremiah 8:4

And now at length discerning 763*
the evil that I do,
behold me, Lord, returning
with hope and trust to you.
In haste you come to meet me
and home rejoicing bring,
in gladness there to greet me
with calf and robe and ring.

The apostles said to the Lord, "Increase our faith!" Luke 17:5

Unseal our lips to sing your praise 561
in endless hymns through all our days;
increase our faith and light our minds;
and set us free from doubt that blinds.

Almighty God, we confess our sins before you this day. Forgive us and turn us toward you, we pray. Just as your apostles asked, we ask you to increase our faith, so that we too may experience your abundant acts of grace and love. In Jesus' name, we pray. Amen.

Saturday, July 1 — Psalm 80:8–11
Isaiah 14; Ephesians 1:1–10

Lord, to you I have committed my cause. Jeremiah 11:20

Lord, I would clasp thy hand in mine, 787
nor ever murmur nor repine,
content, whatever lot I see,
since 'tis my God that leadeth me.

Jesus said, "Your will be done, on earth as it is in heaven." Matthew 6:10

You have kindly led us p205
through our joys and tears;
now accept our praises and remove our fears.
Grant us all with gladness to obey your voice;
let your will and pleasure be our only choice.

Faithful Guide, you lead us through lush, green pastures, and thorny briar patches. Give us ears to listen for your voice, eyes to see your path, and faith to trust them both. Amen.

Fifth Sunday after Pentecost

Watchword for the week — Happy are the people who know the festal shout, who walk, O Lord, in the light of your countenance. Psalm 89:15

Sunday, July 2 — Jeremiah 28:5-9; Psalm 89:1-4,15-18
Romans 6:12-23; Matthew 10:40-42

The earth, O Lord, is full of your steadfast love; teach me your statutes. Psalm 119:64

Help us, O Lord, to learn 666*
the truths your word imparts:
to study that your laws may be
inscribed upon our hearts.

In everything do to others as you would have them do to you; for this is the law and the prophets. Matthew 7:12

When a poor one who has nothing 689**
shares with strangers,
when the thirsty water give unto us all,
when the crippled in their weakness strengthen others,
then we know that God still goes that road with us,
then we know that God still goes that road with us.

Teacher, your laws are easy to understand but hard for us to live up to—to treat others better than we treat ourselves and to love you most of all. We are trying. Help us to do better. Amen.

Monday, July 3 — Psalm 80:12–19
Isaiah 15,16; Ephesians 1:11–23

Bless the Lord, O my soul, and do not forget all his benefits. Psalm 103:2

Bless the Lord, O my soul! 534*
All within me bless God's name!
Bless the Lord, who was, and is,
and shall ever be the same!
All we need the Lord supplies us
when we walk in paths of truth;
like the eagle, God restores us
to the vigor of our youth.

Give thanks in all circumstances; for this is the will of God in Christ Jesus for you. 1 Thessalonians 5:18

In full thanksgiving for God's love, 451**
from which earth's blessings flow,
protect the precious air above,
the waters spread below.

Gracious Lord, how great are your gifts! Let the praises that flow from our lips serve as the thank you note that we so often forget to send to you. Though we don't always act like it, we are grateful. Help us to show our gratitude to you through our loving actions toward others. Amen.

Tuesday, July 4 — Psalm 81:1–5
Isaiah 17:1–19:17; Ephesians 2:1–10

Those of steadfast mind you keep in peace—in peace because they trust in you. Isaiah 26:3

If you but trust in God to guide you 712
and place your confidence in him,
you'll find him always there beside you
to give you hope and strength within;
for those who trust God's changeless love
build on the rock that will not move.

Now it is God who makes both us and you stand firm in Christ. 2 Corinthians 1:21 NIV

How firm a foundation, you saints of the Lord, 709
is laid for your faith in his excellent word!
What more can he say than to you he has said,
to you who for refuge to Jesus have fled?

Good Shepherd, we are safe with you. You guide, protect, and comfort us—and you will do the same for all you have created. Help us to welcome all into the safety of your fold, to throw wide the gates of your pasture and call out to everyone, shouting, "Come in! Come in! It is safe here!" Amen.

Wednesday, July 5 — Psalm 81:6–10
Isaiah 19:18–22:14; Ephesians 2:11–22

I the Lord do not change. Malachi 3:6

The God of Abraham praise, 468
who reigns enthroned above,
the Ancient of eternal days,
the God of love!
The Lord, the great I Am,
by earth and heav'n confessed—
we bow before his holy name
forever blessed.

His mercy is for those who fear him from generation to generation. Luke 1:50

Triumphant hosts on high 468
give thanks to God and sing,
and "Holy, holy, holy," cry,
"Almighty King!"
Hail, Abraham's God and ours!
One mighty hymn we raise.
All pow'r and majesty be yours
and endless praise!

God of Abraham, you know us—every hair, every freckle. You don't change, but we do. We get older, day by day—new lines, new spots. Yet you still know us—every hair, every freckle. What a gift it is to be known by you. Amen.

John Hus Festival† — Isaiah 49:1-7; Psalm 135:1-13
1 Corinthians 1:18-24; Mark 8:34-38

Thursday, July 6 — Psalm 81:11–16
Isaiah 22:15–23:18; Ephesians 3:1–13

To you, O Lord, I lift up my soul. O my God, in you I trust; do not let me be put to shame. Psalm 25:1-2

For Hus the fearless martyr 391*
we give you thanks and praise,
whose bright and pure example
still shines in these our days.
May we with dedication
so preach and live your love
that all may hear your witness
and strive for heav'n above.

Zacchaeus wanted to see who Jesus was. Luke 19:3 NIV

May the saints of faith's tomorrow 392**
love and trust the God of grace.
May we grow in hopeful living,
may we know God's strong embrace.
We will still by faith move forward,
till we meet God face to face.

Lord Jesus, we pray as Hus prayed, 'O Christ, Son of the living God, have mercy on me.' Hear us, Son of David. Amen.

† On July 6, 1415, John Hus was martyred at the Council of Constance.

Friday, July 7 — Psalm 82:1–4
Isaiah 24,25; Ephesians 3:14–4:6

You have set our iniquities before you, our secret sins in the light of your countenance. Psalm 90:8

Give me your courage, Lord, to speak 686*
whenever strong oppress the weak.
Should I myself as victim live,
rememb'ring you, may I forgive.

And forgive us our debts, as we also have forgiven our debtors. Matthew 6:12

You have cancelled my transgression, p202
Jesus, by your precious blood;
may I find therein salvation,
happiness, and peace with God;
and since you, for sinners suff'ring
on the cross were made an off'ring,
from all sin deliver me,
that I wholly yours may be.

Forgiving God, you have released us from all we owe. How glorious it is to live debt-free! Give us grace to release others in the same way, so that everyone may know the freedom of living without owing anything! Amen.

Saturday, July 8 — Psalm 82:5–8
Isaiah 26,27; Ephesians 4:7–16

The memory of the righteous is a blessing. Proverbs 10:7

Take my life, O Lord, renew, 647
consecrate my heart to you;
take my moments and my days;
let me sing your ceaseless praise.

Do not become sluggish, but imitate those who through faith and patience inherit the promises. Hebrews 6:12 NKJV

Take my love, my Lord, I pour 647
at your feet its treasure store;
take myself, and I will be
yours for all eternity.

Spirit of love, our days are numbered. Help us to use each and every one of them for your purposes. From baptism to burial, equip us to make the most of the time you have given us. Moment by moment, we are yours. Amen.

Sixth Sunday after Pentecost

Watchword for the week — The Lord is gracious and merciful, slow to anger and abounding in steadfast love. Psalm 145:8

Sunday, July 9 — Zechariah 9:9-12; Psalm 145:8-14
Romans 7:15-25a; Matthew 11:16-19,25-30

Their congregation shall be established before me. Jeremiah 30:20

So come by foot or cane or chair 520*
and join with us in song and prayer,
for though we sit or stand in place
our spirits soar and dance with grace.

Paul wrote: If then there is any encouragement in Christ, any consolation from love, any sharing in the Spirit, any compassion and sympathy, make my joy complete: be of the same mind, having the same love, being in full accord and of one mind. Philippians 2:1-2

Christ welcomes all and so do we, 520*
whate'er our limitation be.
Our God in Christ makes all things new,
for God is love unending too.

Welcoming God, we come into your house like children who have been away from home far too long. As we knew you would, you wrap us up in arms of welcome and acceptance. On the table sit our favorite dishes; our bed is made with fresh linens. How wonderful it is to be home—with you! Amen.

Monday, July 10 — Psalm 83:1–8
Isaiah 28; Ephesians 4:17–28

O come, let us worship and bow down, let us kneel before the Lord, our Maker! Psalm 95:6

To you, most holy Lord, 633
we sing with hearts and voices;
in you, with one accord,
your church on earth rejoices!
We bend before your throne
and humbly chant your praise;
we worship you alone,
whose love has crowned our days.

To the King of the ages, immortal, invisible, the only God, be honor and glory forever and ever. 1 Timothy 1:17

All glory, laud, and honor 342
to you, Redeemer, King,
to whom the lips of children
made sweet hosannas ring.
You are the King of Israel
and David's royal Son,
now in the Lord's name coming,
the king and Blessed One.

King of creation, we stand in awe of your creativity. All around us are bursts of color and light that you have knit together in patterns we could never have imagined: symmetry and sequence, spirals and stripes. Animals and plants proclaim your imagination and, along with them, we praise you for your clever artistry. Amen.

Tuesday, July 11 — Psalm 83:9–12
Isaiah 29; Ephesians 4:29–5:7

There is nothing better than that all should enjoy their work, for that is their lot. Ecclesiastes 3:22

O God of ev'ry nation, 683*
of ev'ry race and land,
redeem your whole creation
with your almighty hand;
where hate and fear divide us,
and bitter threats are hurled,
in love and mercy guide us,
and heal our strife-torn world.

Whatever you do, in word or deed, do everything in the name of the Lord Jesus, giving thanks to God the Father through him. Colossians 3:17

Jesus, Master, whom I serve, p42
though so feebly and so ill,
strengthen hand and heart and nerve,
all your bidding to fulfill;
open now my eyes to see
all the work you have for me.

Merciful Lord, we have much to do: redeem the wrongfully accused, bring justice to the oppressed, free the captives, provide for those in need. It's quite a to-do list, but with your help, we'll do all we can. In Jesus' name, we pray. Amen.

Wednesday, July 12 — Psalm 83:13–18
Isaiah 30,31; Ephesians 5:8–20

Spare your people, O Lord, and do not make your heritage a mockery. Joel 2:17

O may your mighty love prevail 374
our sinful souls to spare,
O may we come before your throne
and find acceptance there,
and find acceptance there.

Christ gave himself for us that he might redeem us from all iniquity and purify for himself a people of his own who are zealous for good deeds. Titus 2:14

Endow us richly with your gifts and grace 377
to fit us for the duties of our place;
so open now our lips, our hearts so raise,
that both our hearts and lips may give you praise.

Loving Redeemer, the price you paid for us was so high, we will never understand it. By your wounds, you have healed and restored us to your service. May we fix our eyes on you, so that we can prove to be worthy of your sacrifice. Amen.

Thursday, July 13 — Psalm 84:1–7
Isaiah 32:1–33:16; Ephesians 5:21–33

Reuben said to his brothers, “Shed no blood.” Genesis 37:22

O bless the Lord, my soul! 546
His grace to all proclaim!
And all that is within me join
to bless his holy name.

Always strive to do what is good for each other and for everyone else. 1 Thessalonians 5:15 NIV

We thank you then, O Father, p162
for all things bright and good,
the seed-time and the harvest,
our life, our health, our food;
help us to show thanksgiving for all you freely give;
to love you in our neighbor, and by the way we live.
All good gifts around us are sent from heav’n above;
then thank the Lord, O thank the Lord for all his love.

Peace-giving God, we know that there is never a time when violence is helpful. We will neither shed blood nor harm others. Help us in this commitment—bringing peace to our woeful world and healing to hearts torn by violence. Make us instruments of your perfect peace. Amen.

Friday, July 14 — Psalm 84:8–12
Isaiah 33:17–35:10; Ephesians 6:1–9

You are a people holy to the Lord your God; it is you the Lord has chosen out of all the peoples on earth to be his people, his treasured possession. Deuteronomy 14:2

Joined in community, 514*
treasured and fed,
may we discover
gifts in each other,
willing to lead and be led.

For you are all children of light and children of the day; we are not of the night or of darkness. 1 Thessalonians 5:5

Gracious and holy three, 380
glorious Trinity,
wisdom, love, might:
boundless as ocean's tide
rolling in fullest pride,
through the world far and wide,
let there be light!

Light of the universe, you have chosen us to reflect your light into a darkened world. Make us shine brightly with your love for us and with our love for each other. Amen.

Saturday, July 15 — Psalm 85:1–7
Isaiah 36:1–37:13; Ephesians 6:10–24

God saw my affliction and the labor of my hands. Genesis 31:42

As saints of old their first fruits brought 650*
of vineyard, flock and field
to God, the giver of all good,
the source of bounteous yield;
so we today our first fruits bring,
the wealth of this good land,
of farm, and market, shop and home,
of mind, and heart, and hand.

Paul wrote: You know that in the Lord your labor is not in vain. 1 Corinthians 15:58

Bless, Lord, the labor we bring to serve you, p156**
that with our neighbor we may be fed.
Sowing or tilling, we would be with you,
harvesting, milling for daily bread.

Holy Master, sometimes it seems the laborers are very few. The field is ripe, and we are willing to work, Lord, but it can be discouraging when we think we are working the rows alone. Send us co-laborers to share in the jobs that must be done, so we can work cheerfully together to further your Kin-dom. Amen.

Seventh Sunday after Pentecost

Watchword for the week — There is therefore now no condemnation for those who are in Christ Jesus. Romans 8:1

Sunday, July 16 — Isaiah 55:10-13; Psalm 65:(1-8),9-13
Romans 8:1-11; Matthew 13:1-9,18-23

The Lord God will wipe away the tears from all faces. Isaiah 25:8

Sing praise to God who reigns above, 537
the God of all creation,
the God of pow'r, the God of love,
the God of our salvation.
My soul with comfort rich he fills,
and ev'ry grief he gently stills:
to God all praise and glory!

Jesus said, "Your grief will turn to joy." John 16:20 NIV

When we seek relief 799
from a long-felt grief,
when temptations come alluring,
make us patient and enduring;
show us that bright shore
where we weep no more.

Divine Comforter, sometimes tears overtake us in the strangest places. We weep for those we have lost through distance, or death, or destroyed relationships. Our broken hearts cry out to you. Thank you for being the shoulder we can always cry upon, and the friend whom we can always count on. Amen.

Monday, July 17 — Psalm 85:8–13
Isaiah 37:14–38; Philippians 1:1–11

Though I write the multitude of my instructions, they are regarded as a strange thing. Hosea 8:12

In the bulb there is a flower; 797*
in the seed, an apple tree;
in cocoons, a hidden promise:
butterflies will soon be free!
In the cold and snow of winter
there's a spring that waits to be,
unrevealed until its season,
something God alone can see.

Jesus said, "Everyone then who hears these words of mine and acts on them will be like a wise man who built his house on rock." Matthew 7:24

In our end is our beginning; 797*
in our time, infinity;
in our doubt there is believing;
in our life, eternity.
In our death, a resurrection;
at the last, a victory,
unrevealed until its season,
something God alone can see.

Holy Mystery, we plant seeds for trees under whose shade we may never sit. Water them and fertilize them, groom them and grow them for your glory. Your Kin-dom come, your will be done. Amen.

Tuesday, July 18 — Psalm 86:1–10
Isaiah 38:1–40:5; Philippians 1:12–22

Praise him for his acts of power; praise him for his surpassing greatness. Psalm 150:2 NIV

Eternal are your mercies, Lord; 551
eternal truth attends your word:
your praise shall sound from shore to shore
till suns shall rise and set no more.

Ever since the creation of the world his eternal power and divine nature, invisible though they are, have been understood and seen through the things he has made. Romans 1:20

Each little flow'r that opens, 467
each little bird that sings—
God made their glowing colors,
God made their tiny wings.

Imaginative Creator, we marvel at the great things you have created and repent for the damage we have done to them. We commit to do better, to become more conscientious caregivers, and to encourage others to do the same. Make us a blessing to the earth and to you. Amen.

Wednesday, July 19 — Psalm 86:11–17
Isaiah 40:6–41:7; Philippians 1:23–2:4

God, remember your congregation, which you acquired long ago, which you redeemed to be the tribe of your heritage. Psalm 74:2

Bless, O Lord, this congregation, 442*
gather us within your fold;
may we walk in love before you
as your saints in days of old.
Grant your peace to rest upon us;
let our prayers to you be heard;
speak salvation to our spirits
as you promised in your word.

Jesus said, "For where two or three are gathered in my name, I am there among them." Matthew 18:20

We entreat, we entreat, 528
Lord, lift up your countenance
on your ransomed congregations;
grace to ev'ry soul dispense.
May we in our situations
daily in your great salvation share.
Hear our prayer, hear our prayer.

God, whether we gather online, in-person, or outdoors, we know you are with us. Thank you for your everlasting-presence that can transcend any form of communication. Be present in our pews, our classrooms, and our virtual spaces. Amen.

Thursday, July 20 — Psalm 87
Isaiah 41:8–42:9; Philippians 2:5–18

My salvation and my honor depend on God. Psalm 62:7 NIV

Come, thou fount of ev'ry blessing, 782
tune my heart to sing thy grace;
streams of mercy, never ceasing,
call for songs of loudest praise.
Teach me some melodious sonnet,
sung by flaming tongues above.
Praise the mount—I'm fixed upon it—
mount of God's redeeming love.

Jesus said to her, "Daughter, your faith has made you well; go in peace." Luke 8:48

O, to grace how great a debtor 782
daily I'm constrained to be!
Let that grace, Lord, like a fetter,
bind my wand'ring heart to thee.
Prone to wander, Lord, I feel it,
prone to leave the God I love,
here's my heart, O take and seal it;
seal it for thy courts above.

Lover of our souls, how is it that you cherish even us? We cannot be completely faithful nor completely good, yet you make us well. You send us forth in the peace of your love. Our wandering hearts rest in you. Amen.

Friday, July 21 — Psalm 88:1–5
Isaiah 42:10–43:21; Philippians 2:19–30

When the song was raised, with trumpets and cymbals and other musical instruments, in praise to the Lord, "For he is good, for his steadfast love endures forever," the glory of the Lord filled the house of God. 2 Chronicles 5:13,14

We've a song to be sung to the nations, 621
that shall lift their hearts to the Lord,
a song that shall conquer evil
and shatter the spear and sword,
and shatter the spear and sword.

The holy city, the new Jerusalem, has no need of sun or moon to shine on it, for the glory of God is its light, and its lamp is the Lamb. Revelation 21:2,23

Jerusalem the golden, 814
descending from above,
the city of God's presence,
the vision of God's love—
I know not, O I know not
what joys await us there,
what radiancy of glory,
what bliss beyond compare!

Blessed Architect, what a home you have prepared for us! The light never dims, the music never ends. In it is found no evil, nor darkness, nor crying, nor pain. Best of all, we will be with you. Prepare our hearts for the day when we become heavenly citizens. Amen.

Saturday, July 22 — Psalm 88:6–12
Isaiah 43:22–44:23; Philippians 3:1–11

This is the Lord for whom we have waited; let us be glad and rejoice in his salvation. Isaiah 25:9

This day is holy to the Lord; 821
this day the Lord has made;
we will rejoice with one accord
and in his name be glad.
Come, let us worship and bow down,
with thanks appear before his throne;
he to our songs of praise and prayer
will lend a gracious ear.

Now faith is the assurance of things hoped for, the conviction of things not seen. Hebrews 11:1

I am thine, O Lord—I have heard thy voice, 607
and it told thy love to me;
but I long to rise in the arms of faith
and be closer drawn to thee.

Wounded Healer, you never lead us with guilt, shame, or fear, but with your persistent love. May we be leaders who model your style, drawing others closer to you through loving kindness. Amen.

Eighth Sunday after Pentecost

Watchword for the week — Thus says the Lord, the King of Israel, and his Redeemer, the Lord of hosts: I am the first and I am the last; besides me there is no god. Isaiah 44:6

Sunday, July 23 — Isaiah 44:6-8; Psalm 86:11-17
Romans 8:12-25; Matthew 13:24-30,36-43

You bless the righteous, O Lord; you cover them with favor as with a shield. Psalm 5:12

Now God be with us, for the night is closing, 575
the light and darkness are of his disposing;
and 'neath his shadow here to rest we yield us,
for he will shield us.

The one who was born of God protects them, and the evil one does not touch them. 1 John 5:18

Let holy thoughts be ours 575
when sleep o'ertakes us;
our earliest thoughts be yours when morning wakes us;
for your dear presence will not leave those lonely
who seek you only.

Lord, we will lie down in peace and rest in safety for you are our ever-present protector. Whether we are threatened by foes real or imagined, we will rest in the shadow of your wings. Nightmares have no power over us when you stand ready to scatter them away. When morning comes, we will thank you for never leaving us. Amen.

Monday, July 24 — Psalm 88:13–18
Isaiah 44:24–45:25; Philippians 3:12–4:1

He leads me in right paths for his name's sake. Psalm 23:3

My soul he doth restore again, 720
and me to walk doth make
within the paths of righteousness,
e'en for his own name's sake;
within the paths of righteousness,
e'en for his own name's sake.

I am the good shepherd. I know my own and my own know me. John 10:14

Gentle Jesus, hear our prayer. 574
Keep us in your loving care;
and when evening shadows fall,
casting darkness over all,
loving Jesus, then be near,
for with you we have no fear.

Good Shepherd, when we look around, we see fellow sheep of all shapes, colors, and sizes. Help us to feel welcome with our sisters and brothers, and to welcome others. We are all yours. Amen.

Tuesday, July 25 — Psalm 89:1–8
Isaiah 46:1–48:6; Philippians 4:2–13

I will thank you in the great congregation; in the mighty throng I will praise you. Psalm 35:18

To God all glory, praise, and love 548
be now and ever giv'n
by saints below and saints above,
the church in earth and heav'n.

Sing psalms and hymns and spiritual songs among yourselves, singing and making melody to the Lord in your hearts. Ephesians 5:19

Through all the passing years, O Lord, 512
grant that, when church bells are ringing,
many may come to hear God's word
where he this promise is bringing:
"I know my own, my own know me,
you, not the world, my face shall see;
my peace I leave with you." Amen.

True Foundation, we fling wide open the doors of our churches, so all may come in and join us in our praise of you. We will not bar the doors to anyone and if they do not come to us, we will go to them. Make us your messengers. Amen.

Wednesday, July 26 — Psalm 89:9–18
Isaiah 48:7–49:21; Philippians 4:14–23

[Adam and Eve] hid themselves from the presence of the Lord God. Genesis 3:8

Purge our souls of selfishness. 760*
Cleanse our hearts of bitterness.
Lead us back to righteousness.
Save us, Lord, O save us still.

There is no fear in love, but perfect love casts out fear. 1 John 4:18

The church is God's abiding place, 439
his altar is within,
and here by faith we see God's face,
are cleansed from stain of sin.
A sanctuary for the soul,
where love can cast out fear,
where broken spirits are made whole,
for God himself is here.

Lord God, we admit that sometimes we are afraid of you. We hide from your presence and cower in fear—behind our work, behind our piety, behind our self-righteousness. Amen.

Thursday, July 27 — Psalm 89:19–29
Isaiah 49:22–51:16; Colossians 1:1–14

I, I am the Lord, and besides me there is no savior. Isaiah 43:11

Immortal, invisible, God only wise, 457
in light inaccessible hid from our eyes,
most blessed, most glorious, O Ancient of Days,
almighty, victorious, your great name we praise.

And this is eternal life, that they may know you, the only true God, and Jesus Christ whom you have sent. John 17:3

Let all mortal flesh keep silence, p184
and with fear and trembling stand,
ponder nothing earthly minded,
for with blessing in his hand
Christ our God to earth descended,
our full homage to demand.

God, we are listening. Meet us in the silence... Amen.

Friday, July 28 — Psalm 89:30–37
Isaiah 51:17–53:12; Colossians 1:15–27

You who love the Lord, hate evil! Psalm 97:10 NKJV

God his own shall tend and nourish, 667*
in his holy courts they flourish.
From all evil pow'rs he spares them;
in his mighty arms he bears them.

You cannot serve God and wealth. Matthew 6:24

God has given, he has taken, 667*
but his children ne'er forsaken;
his the loving purpose solely
to preserve them pure and holy.

God, we abhor the things that hurt your beloved children: poverty, violence, racism, hatred. Make us agents to stop them. Enable us to bind up the wounded and the hurting and carry them to you. Amen.

Saturday, July 29 — Psalm 89:38–45
Isaiah 54,55; Colossians 1:28–2:10

In the day of my trouble I seek the Lord; in the night my hand is stretched out without wearying. Psalm 77:2

In heav'nly love abiding, 732
no change my heart shall fear;
and safe is such confiding,
for nothing changes here.
The storm may roar around me,
my heart may low be laid,
but God is round about me,
and can I be dismayed?

Jesus said to the disciples, "I am deeply grieved, even to death; remain here, and stay awake with me." And going a little farther, he threw himself on the ground and prayed. Matthew 26:38-39

O Lord, hear my prayer, 745
O Lord, hear my prayer:
when I call answer me.
O Lord, hear my prayer,
O Lord, hear my prayer.
Come and listen to me.

Rabbi, we will pray with you. We are sleepy, and we are weary, but we love you too much to leave you alone. We will cry out through the night. "Abba! Father! Hear us!" Amen.

Ninth Sunday after Pentecost

Watchword for the week — God, turn to me and be gracious to me, as is your custom toward those who love your name. Psalm 119:132

Sunday, July 30 — 1 Kings 3:5-12; Psalm 119:129-136
Romans 8:26-39; Matthew 13:31-33,44-52

When I told of my ways, you answered me; teach me your statutes. Psalm 119:26

O teach me, Lord, that I may teach 646
the precious truths which you impart.
And wing my words that they may reach
the hidden depths of many a heart.

If we know that he hears us in whatever we ask, we know that we have obtained the requests made of him. 1 John 5:15

Are we weak and heavy laden, 743
cumbered with a load of care?
Precious Savior, still our refuge,
take it to the Lord in prayer!
Do your friends despise, forsake you?
Take it to the Lord in prayer!
In his arms he'll take and shield you;
you will find a solace there.

Precious Friend, wherever you would have us go, we will go. Whatever you would have us do, we will do. Whomever you would have us welcome, we will receive. We ask only that you reveal yourself and your will to us. In Jesus' name, we pray. Amen.

Monday, July 31 — Psalm 89:46–52
Isaiah 56,57; Colossians 2:11–23

Do not remember the sins of my youth or my transgressions; according to your steadfast love remember me, for your goodness' sake, O Lord! Psalm 25:7

O Lord of all the living, 763*
both banished and restored,
compassionate, forgiving
and ever caring Lord,
grant now that my transgressing,
my faithlessness may cease.
Stretch out your hand in blessing,
in pardon and in peace.

Jesus said to Nicodemus, "Do not be astonished that I said to you, 'You must be born from above.'" John 3:7

Water has touched us, 408**
fresh on our foreheads,
showing an inward,
spiritual grace.
Into God's fam'ly,
we have been welcomed.
As sons and daughters,
we take our place.

We thank you, gracious God, for the gift of water. Send your Spirit upon us. Bring us into your covenant. We are beloved because you have called us so. Every time we touch the water, may we be reminded of your promise. Amen.

Tuesday, August 1 — Psalm 90
Isaiah 58,59; Colossians 3:1–11

For me it is good to be near God; I have made the Lord God my refuge, to tell of all your works. Psalm 73:28

Other refuge have I none; 724
hangs my helpless soul on thee;
leave, ah, leave me not alone,
still support and comfort me.
All my trust on thee is stayed,
all my help from thee I bring;
cover my defenseless head
with the shadow of thy wing.

He entered the temple with [Peter and John], walking and leaping and praising God. Acts 3:8

Should not I for gladness leap, 662
led by Jesus as his sheep?
For when these blessed days are over
to the arms of my dear Savior
I shall be conveyed to rest.
Amen, yea, my lot is blessed.

God, when we talk about you and your goodness, we do feel closer to you and know you as our strength and our refuge. May we never keep to ourselves what we have experienced of your love and your care. Amen.

Wednesday, August 2 — Psalm 91:1–8
Isaiah 60,61; Colossians 3:12–25

Out of my distress I called on the Lord; the Lord answered me and set me in a broad place. Psalm 118:5

Out of the depths I cry to you; 761*
O Father, hear me calling.
Incline your ear to my distress
in spite of my rebelling.
Do not regard my sinful deeds.
Send me the grace my spirit needs;
without it I am nothing.

Paul wrote: Our hope for you is unshaken; for we know that as you share in our sufferings, so also you share in our consolation. 2 Corinthians 1:7

My hope is built on nothing less 771
than Jesus' blood and righteousness;
no merit of my own I claim
but wholly lean on Jesus' name.

Never, O God, did you promise that your followers would not suffer—just the opposite! Yet you promise to walk beside us in our suffering and to console us with your presence and love. Thank you. In Jesus' holy name, we pray. Amen.

Thursday, August 3 — Psalm 91:9–16
Isaiah 62,63; Colossians 4:1–9

Your love is like the dew that goes away early. Hosea 6:4

Your bountiful care what tongue can recite? 566
It breathes in the air; it shines in the light;
it streams from the hills; it descends to the plain,
and sweetly distills in the dew and the rain.

If I speak in the tongues of mortals and of angels, but do not have love, I am a noisy gong or a clanging cymbal. 1 Corinthians 13:1

Though I may speak with bravest fire, 590*
and have the gift to all inspire,
and have not love: my words are vain
as sounding brass, and hopeless gain.

As we long to grow in love for you, Lord, let us seek to be more like you, loving all people and all creation as you do. Amen.

Friday, August 4 — Psalm 92:1–8
Isaiah 64,65; Colossians 4:10–1 Thessalonians 1:5a

Never be rash with your mouth, nor let your heart be quick to utter a word before God, for God is in heaven, and you upon earth; therefore let your words be few. Ecclesiastes 5:2

Keep me from saying words 615
that later need recalling;
guard me, lest idle speech
may from my lips be falling;
but when, within my place,
I must and ought to speak,
then to my words give grace,
lest I offend the weak.

Do not judge, so that you may not be judged. Matthew 7:1

Pardon, Lord, and are there those 779
who my debtors are, or foes?
I, who by forgiveness live,
here their trespasses forgive.

Lord, govern our speech and our thought, that we may be slow to speak, slow to judge another person, and always quick to love and to forgive. Amen.

Saturday, August 5 — Psalm 92:9–15
Isaiah 66–Jeremiah 1:7; 1 Thessalonians 1:5b–2:9

Give ear to my words, O Lord; give heed to my sighing. Listen to the sound of my cry, for to you I pray. Psalm 5:1-2

O God of grace, we come to you 750
with broken, contrite hearts;
give what your eye delights to view,
truth in the inward parts.

Whatever you ask for in prayer, believe that you have received it, and it will be yours. Mark 11:24

Come now, O Lord, and teach us how to pray. 742
Teach us to ask ourselves from day to day
if we are yours and yours alone will be
through earthly days and through eternity.

Savior, we come to you in prayer at your invitation because you draw us to you. Let us listen to you knowing that you are listening to us. Hear our prayer and speak to our listening hearts. Amen.

Tenth Sunday after Pentecost

Watchword for the week — The Lord is good to all, and his compassion is over all that he has made. Psalm 145:9

Sunday, August 6 — Isaiah 55:1-5; Psalm 145:8-9,14-21
Romans 9:1-5; Matthew 14:13-21

In you our ancestors trusted; they trusted, and you delivered them. Psalm 22:4

Sing, pray, and keep his ways unswerving, 712
offer your service faithfully,
and trust his word; though undeserving,
you'll find his promise true to be.
God never will forsake in need
the soul that trusts in him indeed.

The Lord is compassionate and merciful. James 5:11

Praise to the Savior for his deep compassion, 383
graciously caring for his chosen people;
young men and women, aging folk and children,
praise to the Savior!

Jesus, we remember those in our past who trusted in your compassion and mercy. We long faithfully to rely on you, for we know that whatever we face, you walk with us in strong compassion. With thanks, we pray. Amen.

Monday, August 7 — Psalm 93
Jeremiah 1:8–2:19; 1 Thessalonians 2:10–20

Joseph remained there in prison. But the Lord was with him. Genesis 39:20,21

Long my imprisoned spirit lay 773
fast bound in sin and nature's night.
Your sunrise turned that night to day;
I woke—the dungeon flamed with light!

About midnight Paul and Silas were praying and singing hymns to God, and the prisoners were listening to them. Acts 16:25

My chains fell off, your voice I knew; 773
was freed, I rose, and followed you.
My chains fell off, your voice I knew;
was freed, I rose, and followed you.

In whatever situation we may find ourselves in life, dear Lord, may we remember and bear witness that you are with us. Comfort those in prison and lead us to serve them in your name. Amen.

Tuesday, August 8 — Psalm 94:1–11
Jeremiah 2:20–3:13; 1 Thessalonians 3

My people shall be satisfied with my bounty, says the Lord. Jeremiah 31:14

> Come, you thirsty, come and welcome, 765
> God's free bounty glorify;
> true belief and true repentance,
> ev'ry grace that brings you nigh.

Like good stewards of the manifold grace of God, serve one another with whatever gift each of you has received. 1 Peter 4:10

> In mercy, Lord, this grace bestow, 643
> that in your service we may do
> with gladness and a willing mind
> whatever is for us assigned.

God, may we always respond thoughtfully and carefully to your generosity, knowing that you have entrusted us with gifts, by your grace, for the good of others as well as ourselves. Amen.

Wednesday, August 9 — Psalm 94:12–23
Jeremiah 3:14–4:22; 1 Thessalonians 4:1–12

Great peace have those who love your law; nothing can make them stumble. Psalm 119:165

From your house when I return, 553
may my heart within me burn,
and at evening let me say,
"I have walked with God today."

Let the word of Christ dwell in you richly; teach and admonish one another in all wisdom. Colossians 3:16

I bind unto myself today p237
the power of God to hold and lead,
his eye to watch, his might to stay,
his ear to hearken to my need,
the wisdom of my God to teach,
his hand to guide, his shield to ward;
the word of God to give me speech,
his heavenly host to be my guard.

Spirit of truth, your teachings fill us, surround us, and nourish us all our days. We seek to love your truth, and to share it with one another with the wisdom and gentleness that can come only from you. We pray, in Jesus' name. Amen.

Thursday, August 10 — Psalm 95
Jeremiah 4:23–5:25; 1 Thessalonians 4:13–5:3

Look at the proud! Their spirit is not right in them, but the righteous live by their faith. Habakkuk 2:4

Help then, O Lord, our unbelief; 713
and may our faith abound
to call on you when you are near
and seek where you are found:

Therefore rid yourselves of all sordidness and rank growth of wickedness, and welcome with meekness the implanted word that has the power to save your souls. James 1:21

How silently, how silently, 282
the wondrous gift is giv'n!
So God imparts to human hearts
the blessings of his heav'n.
No ear may hear his coming,
but in this world of sin,
where meek souls will receive him still,
the dear Christ enters in.

Loving God, may we live ever closer to the truth: about you, about others, and about ourselves. Cleanse our hearts and minds daily, dear Lord. Strengthen our faith that we may continue to grow in love and hope. Amen.

Friday, August 11 — Psalm 96:1–9
Jeremiah 5:26–6:30; 1 Thessalonians 5:4–15

God knows what is in the darkness, and light dwells with him. Daniel 2:22

Light of light, we humbly pray, 276*
shine upon your world today;
break the gloom of our dark night,
fill our souls with love and light,
give your blessed word rebirth,
"Peace, good will to all on earth."

The light shines in the darkness. John 1:5

Morning Star, my soul's true light, 281
tarry not, dispel my night.
Morning Star, my soul's true light,
tarry not, dispel my night.
Jesus mine, in me shine;
in me shine, Jesus mine;
fill my heart with light divine.

Light of the world, in summer we forget how dark the winter nights can be. In our happy times, we forget how grim the difficult times can be. In our hardest hours, be our light; in easier times, may we be bearers of your light. Amen.

Saturday, August 12 — Psalm 96:10–13
Jeremiah 7; 1 Thessalonians 5:16–28

My heart exults in the Lord. 1 Samuel 2:1

Grant that we may love you truly; p67
Lord, our thoughts and actions sway,
and to ev'ry heart more fully
your atoning pow'r display.

Rejoice that your names are written in heaven. Luke 10:20

Bring near your great salvation, 394
O Lamb for sinners slain;
fill up the roll of your elect,
then take your pow'r, and reign!
Appear, Desire of nations,
your exiles long for home;
show in the heav'n your promised sign;
then, Prince and Savior, come.

God of strength, God of love, may we today celebrate not our circumstances, but rather the joy of your strength, the constancy of your love, and the certainty that you hold us in your everlasting care. Amen.

Eleventh Sunday after Pentecost

Watchword for the week — Jesus spoke to the disciples and said, "Take heart, it is I; do not be afraid." Matthew 14:27

August Thirteenth Festival† — Joshua 24:16-24; Psalm 133
1 John 4:1-13; John 17:1-2,6-19

Sunday, August 13 — 1 Kings 19:9-18; Psalm 85:8-13
Romans 10:5-15; Matthew 14:22-33

God does great things beyond understanding, and marvelous things without number. Job 9:10

O worship the King, all glorious above, 566
O gratefully sing his power and his love;
our shield and defender, the ancient of days,
pavilioned in splendor, and girded with praise.

Blessed be the God and Father of our Lord Jesus Christ, who has blessed us in Christ with every spiritual blessing in the heavenly places. Ephesians 1:3

To you our vows with sweet accord, 677
head of your church, we pay;
we and our house will serve you, Lord;
your word we will obey.
Grant us and all our children grace
in word and deed your name to praise,
and in each family, your will
and purpose to fulfill.

Spirit of Christ, you can unite people in you, even in our differences. Fill our vision with the sacrifice and love of Jesus, and fill our hearts with love for Jesus, that we may boundlessly love each other. Amen.

† On this date in 1727 in Berthelsdorf, Saxony (now Germany), a group of quarreling Christians experienced their unity in Christ through the power of the Holy Spirit. This new Pentecost marked the revival of the Unity of the Brethren, begun in 1457, and the beginning of the Renewed Moravian Church.

Monday, August 14 — Psalm 97:1–6
Jeremiah 8:1–9:9; 2 Thessalonians 1

Speak out for those who cannot speak, for the rights of all the destitute. Proverbs 31:8

God's word forever shall abide, 788*
no thanks to foes who fear it;
for God himself fights by our side
with weapons of the Spirit.
Were they to take our house,
goods, honor, child, or spouse,
though life be wrenched away,
they cannot win the day.
The kingdom's ours forever.

Remember those who are in prison, as though you were in prison with them; those who are being tortured, as though you yourselves were being tortured. Hebrews 13:3

Blessed are they who show their mercy 595
to the guilty and the poor,
for to them, set free from judgment,
shall be opened heaven's door.
Blessed, the sincere and truthful
from the lie's deception free,
for the God of truth and beauty
they in joy will surely see.

Jesus, you teach that love for you is expressed by loving the least of your brothers and sisters—our brothers and sisters. May we learn to love as you love, and give ourselves as you gave yourself for the life of the world. Amen.

Tuesday, August 15 — Psalm 97:7–12
Jeremiah 9:10–10:16; 2 Thessalonians 2:1–12

When the ways of people please the Lord, he causes even their enemies to be at peace with them. Proverbs 16:7

Lord, cleanse the depths within our souls, 777*
and bid resentment cease;
then, bound to all in bonds of love,
our lives will spread your peace,
our lives will spread your peace.

Love your enemies and pray for those who persecute you, so that you may be children of your Father in heaven. Matthew 5:44-45

Much forgiven, may I learn 779
love for hatred to return;
then my heart assured shall be
you, my God, have pardoned me.

Triune God, we seek to love even those who hurt us, following your words and your actions. It's hard, but we know you are with us to enable us to love beyond our own strength. Amen.

* Used by permission of Oxford University Press.

Wednesday, August 16 — Psalm 98
Jeremiah 10:17–11:23; 2 Thessalonians 2:13–3:5

For we are aliens and transients before you, as were all our ancestors; our days on the earth are like a shadow, and there is no hope. 1 Chronicles 29:15

O come, O come, Immanuel, 274
and ransom captive Israel,
that mourns in lowly exile here
until the Son of God appear.

So we do not lose heart. Even though our outer nature is wasting away, our inner nature is being renewed day by day. 2 Corinthians 4:16

The springs of salvation from Christ, 616
the Rock, bursting
and flowing throughout all the world's wilderness
bring life and salvation to those who are thirsting
to drink from this spring of salvation by grace;
as streams through the desert refresh the ground
and make land once barren with green abound,
the pow'r of his Spirit our cold hearts o'er flowing,
renews us for service with lives bright and glowing.

God of the wilderness, who suffered beyond our comprehension, today we meditate on our life as a pilgrimage and a journey. May we always know you as our creator, our strength, and our everlasting home. Amen.

Thursday, August 17 — Psalm 99
Jeremiah 12:1–13:19; 2 Thessalonians 3:6–18

Gideon said, "I will not rule over you; the Lord will rule over you." Judges 8:23

He rules the world with truth and grace, 294
and makes the nations prove
the glories of his righteousness
and wonders of his love,
and wonders of his love,
and wonders, wonders of his love.

The greatest among you will be your servant. Matthew 23:11

But poor, in weakness, comes the Christ; p58*
his glory gone, no king we see;
a servant, Lord, no praise he seeks.
Thus comes God's power to you and me.

Suffering servant Jesus, may we learn obedience as you did. May we relinquish our desire to be served, our thirst for power, and our hunger for praise. May we look to you and be a witness for you. Amen.

Friday, August 18 — Psalm 100
Jeremiah 13:20–14:22; 1 Timothy 1:1–11

Happy are those who keep his decrees, who seek him with their whole heart. Psalm 119:2

Thus may our lips your praises sound, 519
our hearts in steadfast hope abound;
till you to heaven our steps shall bring
where saints and angels hail you King.

Therefore, whoever breaks one of the least of these commandments, and teaches others to do the same, will be called least in the kingdom of heaven; but whoever does them and teaches them will be called great in the kingdom of heaven. Matthew 5:19

O blessed Lord, teach me your law, 510
your righteous judgments I declare;
your testimonies make me glad,
for they are wealth beyond compare.

Teach us to hear and heed your instruction, Spirit of truth, for therein is our greatest joy and peace. Amen.

Saturday, August 19 — Psalm 101
Jeremiah 15:1–16:13; 1 Timothy 1:12–2:7

You know me, O Lord; you see me; and you examine my heart's attitude toward you. Jeremiah 12:3 NASB

Create in me a clean heart, O God, p79
and renew a right spirit within me.
Cast me not away from your presence,
and take not your Holy Spirit from me.
Restore unto me the joy of salvation;
anoint me with your Spirit free.
Create in me a clean heart, O God,
and renew a right spirit within me.

Speaking the truth in love, we must grow up in every way into him who is the head, into Christ. Ephesians 4:15

Teach us to love in truth, 801*
to give and to receive
with joyful and with open hearts,
with all that we believe;
to seek another's good,
to honor what is right,
to let our will and our desire
be held in holy light.

O holy Wisdom, you know our every thought and feeling. May we grow to maturity and into the image of Christ with all our sisters and brothers together. Amen.

Twelfth Sunday after Pentecost

Watchword for the week — Let the peoples praise you, O God; let all the peoples praise you. Psalm 67:5

Sunday, August 20 — Isaiah 56:1,6-8; Psalm 67
Romans 11:1-2a,29-32; Matthew 15:(10-20),21-28

God said, "Let there be light;" and there was light. Genesis 1:3

Rank on rank the host of heaven 271
spreads its vanguard on the way,
as the Light of light descending
from the realms of endless day,
that the powers of hell may vanish
as the darkness clears away.

The fruit of the light is found in all that is good and right and true. Ephesians 5:9

Christ, whose glory fills the skies, 475
Christ, the true and only light,
Sun of righteousness, arise,
triumph o'er the shades of night;
dayspring from on high, be near;
daystar, in my heart appear.

Creator God, you made all things good. Today may we focus our attention on seeing the good in everything you made, and may our works and words reflect your light clearly and cleanly. Amen.

Monday, August 21† — Psalm 102:1–11
Jeremiah 16:14–17:27; 1 Timothy 2:8–3:7

I will give them a heart to know that I am the Lord. Jeremiah 24:7

Lord, we your presence seek; 584
we ask this blessing true:
give us a pure and lowly heart,
a temple fit for you.

Paul wrote: Pray for us that God will open to us a door for the word, that we may declare the mystery of Christ. Colossians 4:3

Majesty veiled in mystery p100*
as three in one, and one in three,
beyond our scope, and far above,
you have revealed yourself in love.

Wherever we go in the name of Jesus, Holy Spirit, you are there before us. Today let us speak the words you give us, with the heart of love that only you can give. Amen.

† On this day in 1732, the first missionaries departed from Herrnhut bound for St. Thomas.

Tuesday, August 22 — Psalm 102:12–22
Jeremiah 18:1–19:9; 1 Timothy 3:8–16

The Lord your God is testing you, to know whether you indeed love the Lord your God with all your heart and soul. Deuteronomy 13:3

Enrich me always with your love; 733
my kind protector ever prove;
Lord, put your seal upon my heart,
that I from you may not depart.

God is faithful, and he will not let you be tested beyond your strength, but with the testing he will also provide the way out so that you may be able to endure it. 1 Corinthians 10:13

Be still my soul: the Lord is on your side. 757
Bear patiently the cross of grief or pain;
leave to your God to order and provide;
in ev'ry change God faithful will remain.
Be still, my soul: your best, your heav'nly friend
through thorny ways leads to a joyful end.

Caring God, you give what is needed to answer every call. You provide the strength needed to face every challenge. Your presence is the cure for every fear. With awe, we receive your care, strength, and comfort. Amen.

Wednesday, August 23 — Psalm 102:23–28
Jeremiah 19:10–21:10; 1 Timothy 4:1–10

I will recount the gracious deeds of the Lord, the praiseworthy acts of the Lord, because of all that the Lord has done for us. Isaiah 63:7

We thank you, our Creator, 453
for all things bright and good,
the seedtime and the harvest,
our life, our health, our food;
accept the gifts we offer
for all your love imparts,
and what you most would treasure—
our humble, thankful hearts.

Indeed you have tasted that the Lord is good. 1 Peter 2:3

Brothers, sisters, join in praising p193*
Christ, the Son, Incarnate Word;
join, with hearts and voices raising,
songs of thanks to Christ, our Lord.
God made flesh, who dwelt among us
giving bread and wine as sign,
grant that now your love may, through us,
in a world of darkness shine.

All praise to you, God, who acts for the good of your children! May we embrace all people, as you do, as your beloved children, and as our beloved brothers and sisters! Amen.

Thursday, August 24 — Psalm 103:1–5
Jeremiah 21:11–22:30; 1 Timothy 4:11–5:8

The Lord said to me, "You are my servant, Israel, in whom I will be glorified." Isaiah 49:3

Your faithful servants bless 633
in all earth's varied places;
your name they all confess
among earth's many races,
until that day shall come
when multitudes untold
shall find their glorious home
in heav'n's eternal fold!

You know the message God sent to the people of Israel, announcing the good news of peace through Jesus Christ, who is Lord of all. Acts 10:36 NIV

It is by grace we are assured 781*
that we belong to him:
the love we share in Christ our Lord,
the Spirit's work within.

God of Abraham, Isaac, and Jacob, we honor our brothers and sisters of our faith as your chosen people, through Jesus Christ, son of David, in whose name we pray. Amen.

Friday, August 25 — Psalm 103:6–18
Jeremiah 23:1–32; 1 Timothy 5:9–16

I said, "I have toiled in vain, I have spent my strength for nothing and vanity; yet surely the justice due to me is with the Lord, and my reward with my God." Isaiah 49:4 NASB1995

Refresh your people on their toilsome way; p139
lead us from night to never-ending day;
fill all our lives with heav'n-born love and grace,
until at least we meet before your face.

Be patient, therefore, beloved, until the coming of the Lord. The farmer waits for the precious crop from the earth, being patient with it until it receives the early and the late rains. James 5:7

Only be still and wait his pleasure 712
in cheerful hope with heart content.
He fills your needs to fullest measure
with what discerning love has sent;
doubt not our inmost wants are known
to him who chose us for his own.

Teach us, Holy Spirit, to leave final outcomes to you. We see dimly and only what is now. What is to be is in your care. Give us wisdom to act when we should and patience to wait for your guidance. Amen.

Saturday, August 26 — Psalm 103:19–22
Jeremiah 23:33–25:14; 1 Timothy 5:17–6:2

Share your bread with the hungry. Isaiah 58:7

O lead me, Lord, that I may lead 646
the wand'ring and the wav'ring feet.
O feed me, Lord, that I may feed
your hungry ones with manna sweet.

Do not neglect to do good and to share what you have, for such sacrifices are pleasing to God. Hebrews 13:16

New life for some means food and warmth, 481*
for some the right to speak,
for some the comfort of a friend
or loving God to meet.
So help us, Christ, as now we join
with Christians ev'rywhere
to touch and teach, to comfort, feed,
your love the world to share.

Today, God who gave us everything, may we not cling to what we have but share with those who need what we can give. Let us give freely as you have given to us. Amen.

Thirteenth Sunday after Pentecost

Watchword for the week — Do not be conformed to this world, but be transformed by the renewing of your minds, so that you may discern what is the will of God—what is good and acceptable and perfect. Romans 12:2

Sunday, August 27 — Isaiah 51:1-6; Psalm 138
Romans 12:1-8; Matthew 16:13-20

The Lord your God has blessed you in all your undertakings. Deuteronomy 2:7

Show'rs of blessing, show'rs of blessing 636
from the Lord proceed,
strength supplying, strength supplying
in the time of need;
for no servant of our King
ever lacked for anything.
He will never, he will never
break the bruised reed.

From his fullness we have all received, grace upon grace. John 1:16

Chosen flock, your faithful Shepherd follow, 444
who laid down his life for you;
all your days unto his service hallow,
each to be disciples true;
evermore rejoice to do his pleasure,
be the fullness of his grace your treasure;
should success your labor crown,
give the praise to him alone.

Open our eyes, Spirit of truth, to see the grace upon grace you have lavished on us. May we recognize your hand of blessing and may we bless others with your love and mercy. Amen.

Monday, August 28 — Psalm 104:1–9
Jeremiah 25:15–26:9; 1 Timothy 6:3–16

One who rules over people justly, ruling in the fear of God, is like the light of morning, like the sun rising. 2 Samuel 23:3-4

What God's almighty pow'r has made, 537
in mercy he is keeping;
by morning glow or evening shade
his eye is never sleeping.
And where he rules in kingly might,
there all is just and all is right:
to God all praise and glory!

Jesus said, "Take my yoke upon you, and learn from me; for I am gentle and humble in heart, and you will find rest for your souls." Matthew 11:29

The sure provisions of my God 730
attend me all my days;
O may your house be my abode
and all my work be praise.
There would I find a settled rest,
while others go and come—
no more a stranger or a guest,
but like a child at home.

May we stop trying to do everything with our own strength. May we hear your guidance and learn from you, Jesus, our master. Amen.

Tuesday, August 29 — Psalm 104:10–18
Jeremiah 26:10–27:22; 1 Timothy 6:17–2 Timothy 1:7

I am the Lord your God, who teaches you for your own good, who leads you in the way you should go. Isaiah 48:17

Take us under your protection, 716
grant us to obey your voice,
simply follow your direction,
to your will resign our choice.

Mary sat at the Lord's feet and listened to what he was saying. Luke 10:39

O let me hear you speaking 603
in accents clear and still,
above the storms of passion,
the murmurs of self-will.
O speak to reassure me,
to hasten or control;
and speak to make me listen,
O guardian of my soul.

Spirit of wisdom, teach us what you would have us learn. Remind us to sit and listen for your voice in prayer, in quiet meditation, and in the words of sisters and brothers walking with us. Amen.

Wednesday, August 30 — Psalm 104:19–23
Jeremiah 28:1–29:14; 2 Timothy 1:8–18

Lord God, do not destroy the people who are your very own possession, whom you redeemed in your greatness. Deuteronomy 9:26

We are God's house of living stones, 512
built for his own habitation;
he fills our hearts, his humble thrones,
granting us life and salvation.
Yet to this place, an earthly frame,
we come with thanks to praise his name;
God grants his people true blessing.

God who did not withhold his own Son, but gave him up for all of us, will he not with him also give us everything else? Romans 8:32

O love, how deep, how broad, how high, 485
beyond all thought and fantasy,
that God, the Son of God, should take
our mortal form for mortals' sake.

God, you give us your very self, holding nothing back because of your love for us. You conquered death with that love. We worship and adore you. Amen.

Thursday, August 31 — Psalm 104:24–30
Jeremiah 29:15–30:11; 2 Timothy 2:1–13

The Lord gave them food from heaven in abundance. He opened the rock, and water gushed out; it flowed through the desert like a river. For he remembered his holy promise. Psalm 105:40-42

Shepherd of souls, refresh and bless 411
your chosen pilgrim flock
with manna in the wilderness,
with water from the rock.

Give us this day our daily bread. Matthew 6:11

Praise God, from whom all blessings flow; 817
praise him, all creatures here below;
praise him above, ye heavn'ly host;
praise Father, Son, and Holy Ghost! Amen.

Abundance is your very nature, God of all creation—no two snowflakes alike, no two people alike, no two sunrises alike. May we trust in your goodness and your promises, and may we too give in abundance as we have received. Amen.

Friday, September 1 — Psalm 104:31–35
Jeremiah 30:12–31:22; 2 Timothy 2:14–26

You are wearied with your many consultations.
Isaiah 47:13

Breath of God, O life-giving Spirit, 499*
yours the truth that we seek this day.
Yours the wisdom, yours the understanding,
yours the guidance on life's dark way.
Source of courage when hearts are weary,
source of strength for the day's long journey,
Spirit God, our hope and our faith,
breathe now within us your holy breath.

Do not claim to be wiser than you are.
Romans 12:16

Be thou my wisdom, and thou my true word; 719
I ever with thee and thou with me, Lord;
thou my great Father, I thy true son;
thou in me dwelling, and I with thee one.

Gracious God, thank you for your understanding, even when we seek counsel that does not honor your holy truth. Please guide us into the fullness of your presence and power, which are always available to us. Amen.

Saturday, September 2 — Psalm 105:1–7
Jeremiah 31:23–32:15; 2 Timothy 3:1–9

You shall not spread a false report. Exodus 23:1

Hear us, O Lord, as we now pray, 536*
dedicate us to your way;
lead us to work that bears your fruit,
giving knowledge of your truth.
Open our door and enter in,
rescue from darkness and from sin.
Strengthen according to your might,
share with us the promised life.

So then, putting away falsehood, let all of us speak the truth to our neighbors, for we are members of one another. Ephesians 4:25

"Forgive our sins as we forgive," 777**
you taught us, Lord, to pray;
but you alone can grant us grace
to live the words we say,
to live the words we say.

Incarnate Word, our words have power. May we always be mindful of our language and what it conveys in all our conversations today. In Jesus' name, we pray. Amen.

Fourteenth Sunday after Pentecost

Watchword for the week — Jesus said, "If any want to become my followers, let them deny themselves and take up their cross and follow me." Matthew 16:24

Sunday, September 3 — Jeremiah 15:15-21; Psalm 26:1-8
Romans 12:9-21; Matthew 16:21-28

Look down from heaven and see, from your holy and glorious habitation. Where are your zeal and your might? Isaiah 63:15

Then let us adore and give him his right, 565
all glory and pow'r and wisdom and might,
all honor and blessing, with angels above,
and thanks never ceasing for infinite love.

For through the Spirit, by faith, we eagerly wait for the hope of righteousness. Galatians 5:5

While your glorious praise is sung, 553
touch my lips, unloose my tongue
that my joyful soul may bless
Christ the Lord, my righteousness.

Mighty God, bless us today with faith that is eager, hopeful, and trusting. May your righteousness guide us with strength and wisdom. Amen.

Monday, September 4 — Psalm 105:8–15
Jeremiah 32:16–33:5; 2 Timothy 3:10–4:8

My God, my soul is cast down within me; therefore I remember you. Psalm 42:6

Sometimes I feel discouraged, 500
and think my work's in vain,
but then the Holy Spirit
revives my soul again.

I will not leave you orphaned; I am coming to you. John 14:18

Abide with me; fast falls the eventide; 807
the darkness deepens; Lord, with me abide.
When other helpers fail and comforts flee,
help of the helpless, O abide with me.

Abiding God, thank you for your steadfast lovingkindness through the hardest times of our lives. Your warm shelter sustains us more often than we may ever know. Amen.

Tuesday, September 5 — Psalm 105:16–22
Jeremiah 33:6–34:7; 2 Timothy 4:9–22

I have swept away your transgressions like a cloud, and your sins like mist; return to me, for I have redeemed you. Isaiah 44:22

Praise, my soul, the King of heaven, 529
to his feet your tribute bring.
Ransomed, healed, restored, forgiven,
evermore his praises sing.
Alleluia! Alleluia!
Praise the everlasting King!

God erased the record that stood against us with its legal demands. He set this aside, nailing it to the cross. Colossians 2:14

I know not how that Calvary's cross 704
a world from sin could free;
I only know its matchless love
has brought God's love to me.

Gentle One, you generously forgive all our mistakes: how we hurt others, how we walk away from you. Nurture our hearts to savor and share your joy in forgiving others their mistakes and missteps. In Jesus' name, we pray. Amen.

Wednesday, September 6 — Psalm 105:23–36
Jeremiah 34:8–35:19; Titus 1:1–9

Speak the truth to one another, render in your gates judgments that are true and make for peace. Zechariah 8:16

O day of God, draw nigh 681*
in beauty and in pow'r,
come with your timeless judgment now,
to match our present hour.

Let us then pursue what makes for peace and for mutual upbuilding. Romans 14:19

O Christ, who by a cross made peace your sign, 766**
who gives your peace in water, bread and wine:
O Spirit Christ who is our spirit's home,
teach us the secret of the true shalom.

Lord, help us repent from all the ways we resist doing what we know can make peace in and among ourselves. Guide us to speak truth, to make good judgments reflecting your grace. Teach us the power of creating mutual understanding. Amen.

Thursday, September 7 — Psalm 105:37–45
Jeremiah 36; Titus 1:10–2:5

Inquire first for the word of the Lord.
2 Chronicles 18:4

If you but trust in God to guide you 712
and place your confidence in him,
you'll find him always there beside you
to give you hope and strength within;
for those who trust God's changeless love
build on the rock that will not move.

Continue in the things which you have learned and been assured of. 2 Timothy 3:14 NKJV

Holy Lord, holy Lord, 506
thanks and praise be yours, O Lord,
that your word to us is given,
teaching us with love outpoured
that as Lord of earth and heaven,
everlasting life for us to gain,
you were slain, you were slain.

Steadfast Love, may we always consult you about whatever matters to us, because we know we matter to you. May we remember to listen for your responses. We trust you will always be clear and honest with us. In Jesus' name, we pray. Amen.

Friday, September 8 — Psalm 106:1–5
Jeremiah 37:1–38:13; Titus 2:6–3:2

Your dead shall live. Isaiah 26:19

Oh, blessed communion, fellowship divine, 390
we feebly struggle, they in glory shine;
yet all are one within your great design.
Alleluia! Alleluia!

Since we are surrounded by so great a cloud of witnesses, let us also lay aside every weight and the sin that clings so closely. Hebrews 12:1

For all the saints who from their labors rest, 390
who to the world by faith their Lord confessed,
your name, O Jesus, be forever blessed.
Alleluia! Alleluia!

O God, you understand our sorrows and are with us in all our grief, bearing it for us when we cannot. We are grateful that our loved ones who are no longer with us now reside with you. Amen.

Saturday, September 9 — Psalm 106:6–12
Jeremiah 38:14–39:18; Titus 3:3–15

He is mindful of his covenant forever, of the word that he commanded, for a thousand generations. Psalm 105:8

Since we, though unworthy, 746
through electing grace,
'mid your ransomed people
have obtained a place,
Lord, may we be faithful
to our cov'nant found,
to you, as our shepherd,
and your flock fast bound.

The gifts and the calling of God are irrevocable. Romans 11:29

Ye who called, ye who called 636
to Christ's service are,
join together, join together
both in work and prayer;
venture all on him, our Lord,
who assures us in his word,
we are always, we are always
objects of his care.

Everlasting God, your covenant, gifts, and calling are steadfast and irrevocable. We are joined together in community that is centered in the truth of your love for, and commitment to, us forever. We are grateful that we are yours and you are ours. Amen.

Fifteenth Sunday after Pentecost

Watchword for the week — Give me understanding, O God, that I may keep your law and observe it with my whole heart. Psalm 119:34

Sunday, September 10 — Ezekiel 33:7-11; Psalm 119:33-40
Romans 13:8-14; Matthew 18:15-20

God has made me fruitful in the land of my misfortunes. Genesis 41:52

When I walk through the shades of death, 730
your presence is my stay;
one word of your supporting breath
drives all my fears away.
Your hand, in sight of all my foes,
shall still my table spread;
my cup with blessings overflows;
your oil anoints my head.

We also boast in our sufferings, knowing that suffering produces endurance, and endurance produces character, and character produces hope. Romans 5:3-4

We are yours; in love befriend us, 731
be the guardian of our way;
keep your flock, from sin defend us,
seek us when we go astray.
Blessed Jesus, blessed Jesus,
hear your children when we pray.
Blessed Jesus, blessed Jesus,
hear your children when we pray.

Kind, attentive God, none of us is immune to the harsh realities of life. In these hard times, you are present, reliable, and loving. Help us trust and depend on you as our shepherd and the guardian of our way. Amen.

Monday, September 11 — Psalm 106:13–23
Jeremiah 40,41; Philemon 1:1–11

It is better to take refuge in the Lord than to put confidence in mortals. Psalm 118:8

My God will lead me to a spot 794
where, all my cares and griefs forgot,
I shall enjoy sweet rest.
As pants for cooling streams the hart,
I languish for my heavenly part,
for God, for God, my Refuge blessed.

Paul wrote: At my first defense no one came to my support, but all deserted me. May it not be counted against them! But the Lord stood by me and gave me strength. 2 Timothy 4:16-17

Under the shadow of your throne 461
your saints have dwelt secure;
sufficient is your arm alone,
and our defense is sure.

Eternal Protector, when every security falls away, when we stand defenseless, you stand with us. You have loved us with everlasting love; you have drawn us with every kindness. Help us trust your continued assurance no matter what our circumstances. Amen.

Tuesday, September 12 — Psalm 106:24–31
Jeremiah 42,43; Philemon 1:12–25

[The Lord said] "You have seen how I bore you on eagles' wings and brought you to myself." Exodus 19:4

He by his name has sworn, 468
on this we shall depend,
and as on eagles' wings upborne
to heav'n ascend.
There we shall see his face,
his pow'r we shall adore
and sing the wonders of his grace
forevermore.

So do not throw away your confidence; it will be richly rewarded. Hebrews 10:35 NIV

Come, Almighty to deliver, 474
let us all your life receive;
suddenly return, and never,
never more your temple leave.
You we would be always blessing,
serve you as your hosts above,
pray, and praise you without ceasing,
glory in your perfect love.

God, your love upholds us and gives us confidence. Guide and direct us to welcome your power, and to discipline ourselves in applying it in how we think, speak, and act today. Amen.

Wednesday, September 13 — Psalm 106:32–39
Jeremiah 44; Hebrews 1:1–9

In the midst of the congregation I will praise you. Psalm 22:22

Praise to God, immortal praise, p119
for the love which crowns our days!
Bounteous source of every joy,
let your praise our tongues employ,
all to you our God we owe,
source from which all blessings flow.

Jesus prayed for his disciples: "The glory that you have given me I have given them, so that they may be one, as we are one." John 17:22

One our Master, one alone, 525
none but Christ as Lord we own;
"*brethren of his law" are we—
"As I loved you, so love ye."
Branches we in Christ, the Vine,
living by his life divine;
as the Father with the Son,
so, in Christ, we all are one.

As one congregation, we praise your name, faithful Savior. We are grateful for all the ways in which you love us, shown to us so generously in the prayers Jesus offered for his disciples and for us. May your will be done through us today. Amen.

* This was a name applied to itself by the Moravian Church in the fifteenth century.

Thursday, September 14 — Psalm 106:40–48
Jeremiah 45,46; Hebrews 1:10–2:8a

As a father has compassion for his children, so the Lord has compassion for those who fear him. Psalm 103:13

Great is thy faithfulness, O God my Father, 460*
there is no shadow of turning with thee;
thou changest not, thy compassions they fail not;
as thou hast been thou forever wilt be.

Jesus said, "If you then, who are evil, know how to give good gifts to your children, how much more will your Father in heaven give good things to those who ask him!" Matthew 7:11

Pardon for sin and a peace that endureth, 460*
thine own dear presence to cheer and to guide;
strength for today and bright hope for tomorrow,
blessings all mine, with ten thousand beside!

Abundant Giver of life, thank you for your goodness, mercy, and blessings that fill our days to overflowing. May we remember each day that you are the source of all that we are and all that we have. Amen.

Friday, September 15 — Psalm 107:1–9
Jeremiah 47:1–48:25; Hebrews 2:8b–18

My heart recoils within me; my compassion grows warm and tender. I will not execute my fierce anger; for I am God and no mortal, the Holy One in your midst. Hosea 11:8-9

God will not be always chiding, 534*
nor forever angry be;
God will deal with us in mercy,
not according to our sin.

Jesus said, "I came not to judge the world, but to save the world." John 12:47

God removes all our transgressions 534*
far as east is from the west;
for the grace of God is great as
heav'n stands high above the earth!

Merciful One, we find it hard to comprehend that we are created in your image, not the other way around. While we are inclined by our human nature to judge, you, by your divine nature, delight in graciousness. May we remember who made us and to whom we belong. Amen.

Minister's Covenant Day†

Saturday, September 16 — Psalm 107:10–16
Jeremiah 48:26–49:16; Hebrews 3:1–15

You have taken up my cause, O Lord, you have redeemed my life. Lamentations 3:58

For God, in grace and tenderness, 519
regarded us in our distress;
yea, to our aid himself he came;
let all adore God's holy name.

Christ suffered for you, leaving you an example, so that you should follow in his steps. When he was abused, he did not return abuse; when he suffered, he did not threaten; but he entrusted himself to the one who judges justly. 1 Peter 2:21,23

Father in heav'n, fulfill your word; 519
grant us the Spirit of our Lord,
that through your truth, which cannot fail,
we may o'er ev'ry ill prevail.

God, you are all-powerful, and you love us. You always come to help us. You champion our cause, and when we suffer, you hold us safely in your embrace. May we embody Jesus' example of entrusting himself to you in the difficult times. Amen.

† During a synodal conference in London, Jesus Christ was recognized as chief elder of the Brethren's Church. The day is observed as a covenanting day for servants of the church.

Sixteenth Sunday after Pentecost

Watchword for the week — Bless the Lord, O my soul, and do not forget all his benefits. Psalm 103:2

Sunday, September 17 — Genesis 50:15-21; Psalm 103:(1-7),8-13 Romans 14:1-12; Matthew 18:21-35

No inhabitant will say, "I am sick"; the people who live there will be forgiven their iniquity. Isaiah 33:24

Now thank we all our God 533
with heart and hands and voices,
who wondrous things has done,
in whom his world rejoices;
who, from our mother's arms,
has blessed us on our way
with countless gifts of love,
and still is ours today.

Christ said, "Do not be afraid; I am the first and the last, and the living one. I was dead, and see, I am alive forever and ever; and I have the keys of Death and of Hades." Revelation 1:17-18

All praise and thanks to God 533
the Father now be given,
the Son and Spirit blessed,
who reign in highest heaven—
the one eternal God,
whom heav'n and earth adore;
for thus it was, is now,
and shall be evermore.

Most loving God, the certainty of your blessings is eternal, everlasting, from generation to generation. We are grateful and humbled that it is you in whom we live, move, and have our being today. Amen.

Monday, September 18 — Psalm 107:17–22
Jeremiah 49:17–39; Hebrews 3:16–4:5

Know that all lives are mine. Ezekiel 18:4

Let God be God wherever life may be; 459*
let ev'ry tongue bear witness to the call;
all humankind is one by God's decree;
let God be God, let God be God for all.

Paul wrote: I urge that supplications, prayers, intercessions, and thanksgivings be made for everyone. 1 Timothy 2:1

O Lord, hear my prayer, 745
O Lord, hear my prayer:
when I call answer me.
O Lord, hear my prayer,
O Lord, hear my prayer.
Come and listen to me.

Sustaining God, claiming us all as your own, encourage us to come to you with all our hopes, wants, and fears. Teach us that we are worthy of your loving attention. Amen.

Tuesday, September 19 — Psalm 107:23–32
Jeremiah 50:1–40; Hebrews 4:6–16

Trust in him at all times, O people; pour out your heart before him; God is a refuge for us. Psalm 62:8

I fully am persuaded 769
and joyfully declare
I'm never left unaided,
my Father hears my prayer;
his comforts never fail me,
he stands at my right hand;
when tempests fierce assail me,
they're calm at his command.

Now during those days Jesus went out to the mountain to pray; and he spent the night in prayer to God. Luke 6:12

Here, O my Lord, I see you face to face! 421
Here would I touch and handle things unseen,
here grasp with firmer hand eternal grace,
and all my weariness upon you lean.

Eternal Refuge, our trust in you is strengthened when we bring everything in our lives to you in prayer. Please encourage us, welcome us, hear us when we come to you, in whatever state of being we find ourselves. Amen.

Wednesday, September 20 — Psalm 107:33–43
Jeremiah 50:41–51:23; Hebrews 5

In the fear of the Lord one has strong confidence.
Proverbs 14:26

Lord, you have been our dwelling place p147
in every generation.
Your people still have known your grace
and your blessed consolation.
Through every age you heard our cry,
through every age we found you nigh,
our strength and salvation.

Who will separate us from the love of Christ? Will hardship, or distress, or persecution, or famine, or nakedness, or peril, or sword?
Romans 8:35

Lord, nothing from your arms of love p147
shall your own people sever.
Our helper never will remove,
our God will fail us never.
Your people, Lord, have dwelt secure,
our dwelling place you will endure,
forever and forever.

Enduring One, we know you, love you, and serve you. When we feel disconnected from you, please guide our hearts back to the truth, that nothing separates us from you. Thank you, God. Amen.

Thursday, September 21 — Psalm 108:1–5
Jeremiah 51:24–64; Hebrews 6:1–12

You will certainly revere me, you will accept discipline. Zephaniah 3:7 NASB

His sov'reign pow'r without our aid 455
formed us of clay and gave us breath;
and when like wand'ring sheep we strayed,
he saved us from the pow'r of death.

Jesus entered the temple and began to drive out those who were selling things there; and he said, "It is written, 'My house shall be a house of prayer.'" Luke 19:45-46

Called together and united 624*
by the Spirit, we are one.
Hearts and hands are consecrated
to the service of God's Son.
We, entrusted with Christ's mission,
will accept the gracious call.
Faith in action ever, always,
till on earth Christ reigns in all.

Sovereign Lord, your justice is powerful and creative, beginning with each of us allowing your will to work its way in us. We sometimes make the mistake of believing that faithful action takes singular courage. What it takes is union with you and your reconciling purpose in the life of Jesus Christ. On this trust, we base our lives. Amen.

Friday, September 22 — Psalm 108:6–13
Jeremiah 52; Hebrews 6:13–7:3

See, you shall call nations that you do not know, and nations that do not know you shall run to you, because of the Lord your God, the Holy One of Israel, for he has glorified you. Isaiah 55:5

Joyful, joyful, we adore you, 544
God of glory, Lord of love;
hearts unfold like flow'rs before you,
op'ning to the sun above.
Melt the clouds of sin and sadness;
drive the dark of doubt away;
giver of immortal gladness,
fill us with the light of day!

I bow my knees before the Father, from whom every family in heaven and on earth takes its name. Ephesians 3:14-15

Mortals join the mighty chorus, 544
which the morning stars began;
God's own love is reigning o'er us,
joining people hand in hand.
Ever singing, march we onward,
victors in the midst of strife;
joyful music leads us sunward
in the triumph song of life.

Today, dear God, we take in the great mystery of your gathering all people and nations into your family. We are no longer strangers when we worship you and share your love with each other. Thank you, God. Amen.

Saturday, September 23 — Psalm 109:1–7
Lamentations 1:1–15; Hebrews 7:4–17

Do not be discouraged, for you will not suffer disgrace. Isaiah 54:4

"Fear not, I am with you; O be not dismayed, 709
for I am your God and will still give you aid;
I'll strengthen you, help you and cause you to stand
upheld by my righteous, omnipotent hand."

Paul wrote: I do not consider that I have made it my own; but this one thing I do: forgetting what lies behind and straining forward to what lies ahead. Philippians 3:13

Take my hands and let them move 610
at the impulse of your love.
Take my feet and lead their way;
never let them go astray,
never let them go astray.

Constant Spirit, our human actions often lead to broken hearts, wounded pride, and petty grievances that can risk us fracturing our souls and our union with you. Please forgive us our mistakes. Please lift us up by your grace this day, so that we may keep walking with you toward what lies ahead. Amen.

Seventeenth Sunday after Pentecost

Watchword for the week — For to me, living is Christ and dying is gain. Philippians 1:21

Sunday, September 24 — Jonah 3:10-4:11; Psalm 145:1-8
Philippians 1:21-30; Matthew 20:1-16

You shall love your neighbor as yourself: I am the Lord. Leviticus 19:18

Not for tongues of heaven's angels, 591*
not for wisdom to discern,
not for faith that masters mountains;
for this better gift we yearn:
may love be ours, O Lord.

A Samaritan while traveling came near him; and when he saw him, he was moved with pity. He went to him and bandaged his wounds, having poured oil and wine on them. Then he put him on his own animal, brought him to an inn, and took care of him. Luke 10:33-34

Love is humble, love is gentle, 591*
love is tender, true, and kind;
love is gracious, ever-patient,
generous of heart and mind:
may love be ours, O Lord.

You, God, loves us best. We have a lot to learn. Please help us release the fear that stops us from loving fully and deeply in the way that Jesus, our savior, embodied in his life and ministry. Thank you. Amen.

Monday, September 25 — Psalm 109:8–20
Lamentations 1:16–2:10; Hebrews 7:18–28

The word of the Lord is upright, and all his work is done in faithfulness. Psalm 33:4

O Lord our God, 711*
whom all through life we praise,
as year by year, days add to numbered days,
with each we prove the wonders of your ways,
while, still adoring, each new song we raise.

Jesus said, "Heaven and earth will pass away, but my words will not pass away." Matthew 24:35

He leadeth me: O blessed thought! 787
O words with heav'nly comfort fraught!
Whate'er I do, where'er I be,
still 'tis God's hand that leadeth me.

Steadfast, trustworthy God, your words and actions are the same from age to age, and in every generation. You are always reliable, and we can believe and take action in your confident leadership, even when we don't feel so confident ourselves. Thank you, God. Amen.

Tuesday, September 26 — Psalm 109:21–31
Lamentations 2:11–3:15; Hebrews 8

I will exult and rejoice in your steadfast love, because you have seen my affliction; you have taken heed of my adversities. Psalm 31:7

God is love, let heav'n adore him; 463
God is love, let earth rejoice;
let creation sing before him
and exalt him with one voice.
God who laid the earth's foundation,
God who spread the heav'ns above,
God who breathes through all creation:
God is love, eternal love.

Go home to your friends, and tell them how much the Lord has done for you, and what mercy he has shown you. Mark 5:19

I love to tell the story 625
of unseen things above,
of Jesus and his glory,
of Jesus and his love.
I love to tell the story,
because I know it's true;
it satisfies my longings
as nothing else would do.

Love Eternal, your mercy and kindness attend us in days of distress and affliction, peace and joy. May we praise and thank you in all the circumstances of life in which we find ourselves because we know you are with us, sustaining us always. Amen.

Wednesday, September 27 — Psalm 110
Lamentations 3:16–66; Hebrews 9:1–10

In God's hand are the depths of the earth; the heights of the mountains are his also. Psalm 95:4

All things bright and beautiful, 467
all creatures great and small,
all things wise and wonderful—
the Lord God made them all.
The purple-headed mountain,
the river running by,
the sunset, and the morning
that brightens up the sky.

Worship him who made heaven and earth, the sea and the springs of water. Revelation 14:7

All things bright and beautiful, 467
all creatures great and small,
all things wise and wonderful—
the Lord God made them all.
God gave us eyes to see them,
and lips that we might tell
how great is God Almighty,
who has made all things well.

Extravagant Creator, your generosity knows no bounds. May we each take time today to stand still, look around, and take in some of the beauty you share with us in nature and each other. Thank you. Amen.

Thursday, September 28 — Psalm 111
Lamentations 4,5; Hebrews 9:11–22

The Lord will not forsake his people; he will not abandon his heritage. Psalm 94:14

God has given, he has taken, 667*
but his children ne'er forsaken;
his the loving purpose solely
to preserve them pure and holy.

Our citizenship is in heaven, and it is from there that we are expecting a Savior, the Lord Jesus Christ. Philippians 3:20

Faith is a living power from heav'n 700
that grasps the promise God has giv'n,
a trust that can't be overthrown
fixed heartily on Christ alone.

Unchanging Love, when we feel lost, alone, or confused, still our souls to trust in your provision, order, and power. Please strengthen our confidence in you that it may never be shaken. In Jesus' name, we pray. Amen.

Friday, September 29 — Psalm 112
Ezekiel 1,2; Hebrews 9:23–10:4

Let us go with you, for we have heard that God is with you. Zechariah 8:23

Be present with your servants, Lord; 734
we look to you with one accord;
refresh and strengthen us anew,
and bless what in your name we do

How are they to hear without someone to proclaim him? Romans 10:14

Proclaim the gracious word: p138*
God loves the whole wide earth,
to lift, to save, to reconcile,
to grant eternal worth.

Author of all life, may we always delight in sharing our stories of your constant love and abiding presence with those who may not know you. Please continue to draw us close with your kindness, patience, and peace. In Jesus' name, we pray. Amen.

Saturday, September 30 — Psalm 113
Ezekiel 3–4:5; Hebrews 10:5–18

Better is a little with the fear of the Lord than great treasure and trouble with it. Proverbs 15:16

We'll bring him hearts that love him, 658
we'll bring him thankful praise,
and souls forever striving
to follow in his ways:
and these shall be the treasures
we offer to the King,
and these are gifts that even
our grateful hearts may bring.

Keep your lives free from the love of money, and be content with what you have. Hebrews 13:5

Praise to the Lord, 530
who will prosper your work and defend you;
surely his goodness and mercy shall daily attend you.
Ponder anew
what the almighty can do
if with his love he befriend you.

Source of our being, love is a powerful currency of which there is no limit when we rely on you. Please help us steward all our resources, including monetary ones, with that love you so lavishly bestow on us. Amen.

Eighteenth Sunday after Pentecost

Watchword for the week — Let the same mind be in you that was in Christ Jesus. Philippians 2:5

Sunday, October 1 — Ezekiel 18:1-4,25-32; Psalm 25:1-9
Philippians 2:1-13; Matthew 21:23-32

I am the Lord; I act with steadfast love, justice, and righteousness in the earth. Jeremiah 9:24

> Wide as the world is your command, 455
> vast as eternity your love;
> firm as a rock your truth must stand,
> when rolling years shall cease to move

A harvest of righteousness is sown in peace for those who make peace. James 3:18

> All the world is God's own field, 450
> fruit unto his praise to yield,
> wheat and weeds together sown,
> unto joy or sorrow grown;
> first the blade, and then the ear,
> then the full corn shall appear;
> Lord of harvest, grant that we
> wholesome grain and pure may be.

Almighty God, bless us to be blessings unto your creation, your people, and your holy name. Help us to keep Sabbath this day, uniting with sisters and brothers throughout the world, honorably and peaceably. Amen.

Monday, October 2 — Psalm 114
Ezekiel 4:6–6:7; Hebrews 10:19–31

The light of the moon will be like the light of the sun, and the light of the sun will be sevenfold on the day when the Lord binds up the injuries of his people, and heals the wounds. Isaiah 30:26

O come, O bright and morning star, 274
and bring us comfort from afar!
Dispel the shadows of the night,
and turn our darkness into light.

By Christ's wounds you have been healed. 1 Peter 2:24

My lasting joy and comfort here 768
is Jesus' death and blood;
I with this passport can appear
before the throne of God.
Admitted to the realms above,
I then shall see the Christ I love,
where countless pardoned sinners meet
adoring at his feet.

Lord Jesus Christ, son of God, hold us in your divine embrace. Comfort us and heal us. Keep us in the shadow of your mountain and in the sunshine of your love, this day and always. Amen.

Tuesday, October 3 — Psalm 115:1–8
Ezekiel 6:8–7:27; Hebrews 10:32–11:3

Protect me, O God, for in you I take refuge. Psalm 16:1

God is our refuge, strength, and home, 20s*
our help and peace today.
Though pow'rs may fail and sorrows come,
God's light will show the way.

Jesus said, "Do not bring us to the time of trial." Matthew 6:13

Be still and know our Lord is God, 20s*
whose love attends our prayers.
Each whispered word, each silent hope
finds comfort in God's care.

Sometimes our prayers seem selfish and desperate, dear Lord, but you listen anyway. We know you love us and desire to protect us from harm, even though we may question and fear. Let us ponder your goodness and mercy, and give thanks for the many blessings you bestow. Amen.

* by Willie Israel (2010). © 2013 by IBOC and MMF.

Wednesday, October 4 — Psalm 115:9–18
Ezekiel 8,9; Hebrews 11:4–16

The Lord your God is bringing you into a good land, a land with flowing streams, with springs and underground waters welling up in valleys and hills. Deuteronomy 8:7

Jerusalem the golden, 814
descending from above,
the city of God's presence,
the vision of God's love—
I know not, O I know not
what joys await us there,
what radiancy of glory,
what bliss beyond compare!

Barnabas and Paul shouted to the crowds: "God has not left himself without a witness in doing good—giving you rains from heaven and fruitful seasons, and filling you with food and your hearts with joy." Acts 14:17

Here is a pasture, rich and never failing, 593
here living waters in abundance flow;
none can conceive the grace with them prevailing,
who Jesus' shepherd-voice obey and know.
He banishes all fear and strife,
and leads them gently on to everlasting life.

Wise Father, we are filled with desires, but you know our true needs. Teach us to trust your all-sufficient grace. Lead us into mature and abundant life in Christ Jesus. Amen.

Thursday, October 5 — Psalm 116:1–7
Ezekiel 10:1–11:15; Hebrews 11:17–28

Not one of all the good promises that the Lord had made to the house of Israel had failed; all came to pass. Joshua 21:45

Goodness and mercy all my life 720
shall surely follow me,
and in God's house forevermore
my dwelling place shall be;
and in God's house forevermore
my dwelling place shall be.

The entire crowd was rejoicing at all the wonderful things that Jesus was doing. Luke 13:17

Jesus is my joy, 594
therefore blessed am I;
O his mercy is unbounded,
all my hope on him is grounded;
Jesus is my joy,
therefore blessed am I.

You are the source of the smiles on our faces, Lord. You cause our hearts to skip beats. May your holy name, Jesus, be praised, again and again, in every nation. Alleluia, alleluia, alleluia! Amen.

Friday, October 6 — Psalm 116:8–14
Ezekiel 11:16–12:28; Hebrews 11:29–40

Obey me, and I will be your God and you will be my people. Jeremiah 7:23 NIV

My shepherd will supply my need; 730
the Lord God is his name.
In pastures fresh he makes me feed,
beside the living stream.
He brings my wand'ring spirit back
when I forsake his ways,
and leads me for his mercy's sake
in paths of truth and grace.

Jesus said, "If you continue in my word, you are truly my disciples." John 8:31

The sure provisions of my God 730
attend me all my days;
O may your house be my abode
and all my work be praise.
There would I find a settled rest,
while others go and come—
no more a stranger or a guest,
but like a child at home.

Best divine Friend, what a privilege it is to be your covenant people. Thank you for calling us to be your disciples. May we remember you with sincere devotion in everything we do, always. Amen.

Saturday, October 7 — Psalm 116:15–19
Ezekiel 13:1–14:11; Hebrews 12:1–13

Elijah prayed, "Answer me, Lord, answer me, so these people will know that you, Lord, are God, and that you are turning their hearts back again." 1 Kings 18:37 NIV

Lord, speak to me, that I may speak 646
in living echoes of your tone.
As you have sought, so let me seek
your erring children lost and lone.

Jesus said to Peter, "I have prayed for you that your own faith may not fail; and you, when once you have turned back, strengthen your brothers." Luke 22:32

In the hour of trial, 419r
Jesus, plead for me;
lest by base denial
I depart from thee;
when you see me waver,
with a look recall,
nor for fear or favor
suffer me to fall.

We live in a transactional society, Lord, but you call us to be relational people. Open our hearts that we might live, not in isolated self-interest, but as sisters and brothers united in discipleship, reaching out to serve others. In Christ's name, we pray. Amen.

Nineteenth Sunday after Pentecost

Watchword for the week — The stone that the builders rejected has become the chief cornerstone. This is the Lord's doing; it is marvelous in our eyes. Psalm 118:22,23

Sunday, October 8 — Isaiah 5:1-7; Psalm 80:7-15
Philippians 3:4b-14; Matthew 21:33-46

The boundary lines have fallen for me in pleasant places; I have a goodly heritage. Psalm 16:6

As it was without beginning, 458
so it lasts without an end;
to their children's children ever
shall God's righteousness extend.

God is able to provide you with every blessing in abundance, so that by always having enough of everything, you may share abundantly in every good work. 2 Corinthians 9:8

'Tis the most blessed and needful part 768
to have in Christ a share,
and to commit our way and heart
unto his faithful care;
this done, our steps are safe and sure,
our hearts' desires are rendered pure,
and naught can pluck us from his hand,
which leads us to the end.

God, you created us, you love us, and you have plans for us. Why should we worry? Why should we be perplexed? Help us return to you this Sabbath day and abide in you ever more—just as we are, just as you intend. Amen.

Monday, October 9 — Psalm 117
Ezekiel 14:12–15:8; Hebrews 12:14–24

Treasures gained by wickedness do not profit, but righteousness delivers from death. Proverbs 10:2

In haunts of wretchedness and need, 581
on shadowed thresholds dark with fears,
from paths where hide the lures of greed
we catch the vision of your tears.

Zacchaeus said to Jesus, "Look, half of my possessions, Lord, I will give to the poor; and if I have defrauded anyone of anything, I will pay back four times as much." Luke 19:8

Whoe'er would spend their days 593
in lasting pleasure
must come to Christ and join his flock with speed;
here is a feast prepared, rich beyond measure,
the world meanwhile on empty husks must feed.
Those souls may share in ev'ry good
whose Shepherd does possess the treasuries of God.

Christ, we acknowledge that you are the only source of true fulfillment. Deliver us from materialism; free us from the never-ending quest for more. Grant us the peace that comes from surrendering our desires to you. Amen.

Tuesday, October 10 — Psalm 118:1–9
Ezekiel 16:1–42; Hebrews 12:25–13:6

I will leave among you a humble and lowly people, and they will take refuge in the name of the Lord. Zephaniah 3:12 NASB

Faith in the conscience works for peace, 700
and bids the mourner's weeping cease,
by faith the children's place we claim,
and give all honor to one name.

God chose what is low and despised in the world, things that are not, to reduce to nothing things that are, so that no one might boast in the presence of God. 1 Corinthians 1:28-29

Not Jerusalem— 285
lowly Bethlehem
'twas that gave us Christ to save us;
not Jerusalem.

You give us freedom to make choices in life, Lord, and have extended to us an open invitation to turn to you at any time, regardless of circumstance. Move us to choose your way and call upon your holy name, every minute and every hour. Amen.

Wednesday, October 11 — Psalm 118:10–14
Ezekiel 16:43–17:10; Hebrews 13:7–19

Lord, you have been a refuge for the needy in his distress, a shelter from the storm and a shade from the heat. For the breath of the ruthless is like a storm. Isaiah 25:4 NIV

O God, our help in ages past, 461
our hope for years to come,
our shelter from the stormy blast,
and our eternal home!

**While we live, we are always being given up to death for Jesus' sake, so that the life of Jesus may be made visible in our mortal flesh.
2 Corinthians 4:11**

A charge to keep I have, 645
a God to glorify,
a never-dying soul to save
and fit it for the sky.

You are omnipotent, God, yet you delicately care for each of us, even in the small moments of our fragile lives. Remind us today that you believe in us. Let us not forget that, by the spirit, the water, and the blood, you have equipped us to be your disciples. Amen.

Thursday, October 12 — Psalm 118:15–21
Ezekiel 17:11–18:18; Hebrews 13:20–James 1:8

Help me, O Lord my God! Save me according to your steadfast love. Psalm 109:26

'Twas grace that taught my heart to fear 783
and grace my fears relieved;
how precious did that grace appear
the hour I first believed.

When Peter noticed the strong wind, he became frightened, and beginning to sink, he cried out, "Lord, save me!" Jesus immediately reached out his hand and caught him, saying to him, "You of little faith, why did you doubt?" Matthew 14:30-31

Take up your cross, let not its weight 758
fill your weak spirit with alarm;
his strength shall bear your spirit up,
and brace your heart, and nerve your arm.

Lord of our salvation, too often life is difficult, and circumstances leave us feeling alone and filled with fear. Through your grace, you claim us as your own and abide with us in every moment. Embolden us to surrender our anxieties and doubts to you. May we humble ourselves in your presence, which is always with us. Amen.

Friday, October 13 — Psalm 118:22–29
Ezekiel 18:19–19:14; James 1:9–18

He does what he wills with the host of heaven and the inhabitants of the earth. There is no one who can stay his hand or say to him, "What are you doing?" Daniel 4:35

Vainly we offer each ample oblation, 317
vainly with gifts would his favor secure;
richer by far is the heart's adoration,
dearer to God are the prayers of the poor.

Humble yourselves therefore under the mighty hand of God, so that he may exalt you in due time. 1 Peter 5:6

Most holy Lord and God, p203
holy, almighty God,
holy and most merciful Savior,
our eternal God!
Lamb of God unspotted,
to our prayers, O lend an ear.
Have mercy, O Lord.

Discerning God, often we think we are clever and deceive ourselves into believing that we are in control. Sometimes, we even try to subject you to our will, making excuses and offering appeasements. Forgive us, loving Lord. Return us to genuine, forthright faith. Amen.

Saturday, October 14 — Psalm 119:1–8
Ezekiel 20:1–29; James 1:19–27

Lay down a pledge for me with yourself; who is there that will give surety for me? Job 17:3

Were the whole realm of nature mine, 350
that were an off'ring far too small;
love so amazing, so divine
demands my soul, my life, my all.

Who is to condemn? It is Christ Jesus, who died, yes, who was raised, who is at the right hand of God, who indeed intercedes for us. Romans 8:34

How strange is this great paradox to ponder: 351
the shepherd dies for sheep who love to wander;
the master pays the debt his servants owe him,
who would not know him.

Christ Jesus, you are the one and only resurrected Lord who has rendered unto your people the matchless gift of salvation. Guide us as your redeemed followers to respond in the only way we are able, by offering our faith, love, and hope in every aspect of our living. Amen.

Twentieth Sunday after Pentecost

Watchword for the week — O Lord, you are my God; I will exalt you, I will praise your name; for you have done wonderful things. Isaiah 25:1

Sunday, October 15 — Isaiah 25:1-9; Psalm 23
Philippians 4:1-9; Matthew 22:1-14

The righteous know the rights of the poor. Proverbs 29:7

May we now remain in union 441
with each other and the Lord,
and possess, in sweet communion,
joys that earth cannot afford.

Jesus said, "When you give a banquet, invite the poor, the crippled, the lame, and the blind. And you will be blessed, because they cannot repay you." Luke 14:13-14

Feast after feast thus comes and passes by, 421
yet, passing, points to that glad feast above,
giving sweet foretaste of the festal joy,
the Lamb's great marriage feast of bliss and love.

Who are our sisters and brothers, O Lord, but all of your children? Why are the people who discomfort and disquiet us the most usually the ones who help us grow and mature? May we not hesitate to practice radical hospitality as we learn to recognize and honor your divinity in all others. Amen.

Monday, October 16 — Psalm 119:9–16
Ezekiel 20:30–21:17; James 2:1–13

He does not deal with us according to our sins, nor repay us according to our iniquities. Psalm 103:10

O bless the Lord, my soul! 546
His mercies bear in mind!
Forget not all his benefits!
The Lord to all is kind.

Forgive one another, as God in Christ has forgiven you. Ephesians 4:32

May we all so love each other 401*
and all selfish claims deny,
so that each one for the other
will not hesitate to die.
Even so our Lord has loved us;
for our lives he gave his life.
Still he grieves and still he suffers,
for our selfishness and strife.

God with us, it is a wonder that you do not give up on us. By your infinite mercy, may we begin anew to love our neighbors as we love ourselves. Give us courage to surrender our pride and seek forgiveness from those whom we have wronged. Amen.

Tuesday, October 17 — Psalm 119:17–24
Ezekiel 21:18–22:22; James 2:14–26

The Lord will command his angels concerning you to guard you in all your ways. On their hands they will bear you up, so that you will not dash your foot against a stone. Psalm 91:11-12

Perfect submission, perfect delight, 714
visions of rapture now burst on my sight.
Angels descending bring from above
echoes of mercy, whispers of love.

An angel of the Lord appeared to Joseph in a dream and said, "Get up, take the child and his mother, and flee to Egypt, and remain there until I tell you." Matthew 2:13

Lord, who sought by cloak of darkness 692*
refuge under foreign skies
from the swords of Herod's soldiers,
ravaged homes and parents' cries—
may your grace and mercy rest
on the homeless and oppressed.

We acknowledge your protection, good and loving Lord, in our coming and going, night and day. Deepen our conviction in your lovingkindness by helping us perceive that we are, indeed, surrounded by angels. Amen.

Wednesday, October 18 — Psalm 119:25–32
Ezekiel 22:23–23:27; James 3:1–12

I know that the Lord maintains the cause of the needy, and executes justice for the poor. Psalm 140:12

The Lord is never far away, 537
but through all grief distressing,
an everpresent help and stay,
our peace, and joy, and blessing.
As with a mother's tender hand,
he leads his own, his chosen band.
To God all praise and glory!

Blessed are you who are poor, for yours is the kingdom of God. Luke 6:20

Bread of life, bread of life, p146r
Christ, by whom alone we live,
bread that came to us from heaven,
my poor soul can never thrive
unless thou appease its craving;
Lord, I hunger only after thee,
feed thou me, feed thou me.

Compassionate Lord, you have instructed us to care for the poor. Thank you for your teachings about how to serve others. We pray for your assistance in our daily efforts to overcome spiritual poverty—the source of human suffering. Amen.

Thursday, October 19 — Psalm 119:33–40
Ezekiel 23:28–24:8; James 3:13–4:6

The Lord declares, "Those who honor me I will honor, and those who despise me shall be treated with contempt." 1 Samuel 2:30

Holy, holy, holy! 381
Though the darkness hide thee,
though the eye made blind by sin
thy glory may not see,
only thou art holy; there is none beside thee,
perfect in pow'r, in love, and purity.

Or do you despise the riches of his kindness and forbearance and patience? Do you not realize that God's kindness is meant to lead you to repentance? Romans 2:4

To avert from us God's wrath, 416
Jesus suffered in our stead;
by an ignominious death
he a full atonement made;
and by his most precious blood
brought us, sinners, nigh to God.

Our world is filled with ignorance and illusion. As Christians, we are in this world but not of it. Holy Spirit, guide us as we endeavor to illuminate the dark corners, shadows, and voids by sharing in every word and action the good news of God's salvation through Christ. Amen.

Friday, October 20 — Psalm 119:41–48
Ezekiel 24:9–25:14; James 4:7–17

The Lord used to speak to Moses face to face, as one speaks to a friend. Exodus 33:11

From your house when I return, 553
may my heart within me burn,
and at evening let me say,
"I have walked with God today."

Jesus said, "I do not call you servants any longer, because the servant does not know what the master is doing; but I have called you friends, because I have made known to you everything that I have heard from my Father." John 15:15

Jesus, priceless treasure, 722
source of purest pleasure,
friend to me so true,
how my heart has panted
and my soul has fainted,
thirsting after you.
Yours I am, O spotless Lamb,
I will suffer nought to hide you,
nought I ask beside you.

We believe in you, God. You come to us as a personal savior, Jesus, whose name we speak with adoration. You know us, Lord, and you love us with tender affection. With deepest gratitude, we claim you as our dearest friend. Amen.

Saturday, October 21 — Psalm 119:49–56
Ezekiel 25:15–27:11; James 5:1–12

Those who trust in the Lord shall be like a tree planted by water, sending out its roots by the stream. In the year of drought it is not anxious, and it does not cease to bear fruit. Jeremiah 17:7,8

Lifegiving Creator of both great and small; 457
of all life the maker, the true life of all;
we blossom, then wither like leaves on the tree,
but you live forever who was and will be.

The fruit of the Spirit is love, joy, peace, patience, kindness, generosity, faithfulness, gentleness, and self-control. Galatians 5:22-23

Praise the Lord, praise the Lord! 528
He with you deals bounteously.
Highly favored church of Jesus,
he chose you through mercy free
to show forth his matchless praises
and rich fruit, blessed for the Master's use,
to produce, to produce.

Holy Gardener, source of all life, cultivate us this day and nourish us by your Spirit. As deep run the roots of the tree of life, so may our reverence of your grace keep us steadfast, thriving, and bearing good fruit. In Jesus' name, we pray. Amen.

Twenty-first Sunday after Pentecost

Watchword for the week — Sing to the Lord, bless his name; tell of his salvation from day to day. Psalm 96:2

Sunday, October 22 — Isaiah 45:1-7; Psalm 96:1-9,(10-13)
1 Thessalonians 1:1-10; Matthew 22:15-22

You shall not hate in your heart anyone of your kin; you shall reprove your neighbor, or you will incur guilt yourself. Leviticus 19:17

> And in your love may we abide, 519
> estranged from none by wrath or pride,
> among ourselves at unity
> and with all else in charity.

Brothers and sisters, if someone is caught in a sin, you who live by the Spirit should restore that person gently. Galatians 6:1 NIV

> We welcome you among us here, p169
> with joy that God has brought you near.
> With heart and hand we pledge our love,
> and pray Christ's blessing from above.

Lord Jesus, as we attempt to love God's children without condition, may we share kind and respectful words that honor the dignity inherent in others. H-A-T-E is a terrible four-letter word that should never be used, instead may we use the word love, just as you've taught us. Amen.

Monday, October 23 — Psalm 119:57–64
Ezekiel 27:12–28:10; James 5:13–20

He is the living God, enduring forever. His kingdom shall never be destroyed. Daniel 6:26

Holy God, we praise your name: 386
Lord of all, we bow before you.
Saints on earth your rule acclaim;
all in heaven above adore you.
Infinite your vast domain;
everlasting is your reign.

God has put all things under Christ's feet and has made him the head over all things for the church. Ephesians 1:22

Hail, all hail, victorious Lord and Savior, p82
you have burst the bonds of death,
grant us, as to Mary, the great favor
to embrace your feet in faith:
you have in our stead the curse endured,
and for us eternal life procured;
joyful, we with one accord
hail you as our risen Lord.

Christ, our Chief Elder, we are humbled that you have chosen to be our partner in ministry, moving among us and working by our side. We offer anew our talents and energy to further your kingdom on earth. Bless and invigorate your church, we pray. Amen.

Tuesday, October 24 — Psalm 119:65–72
Ezekiel 28:11–29:12; 1 Peter 1:1–12

You have multiplied, O Lord my God, your wondrous deeds and your thoughts towards us; none can compare with you. Psalm 40:5

Praise to the Lord, 530
who o'er all things is wondrously reigning,
shelt'ring you under his wings, O, so gently sustaining.
Have you not seen
all you have needed has been
met by his gracious ordaining.

In Christ are hidden all the treasures of wisdom and knowledge. Colossians 2:3

The word of God, which ne'er shall cease, 509
proclaims free pardon, grace, and peace,
salvation shows in Christ alone,
the perfect will of God makes known.

Author of creation, we marvel at the infinite manifestations of your grace, which surround us and fill our lives to overflowing. We thank you, especially, for the gift of your holy word. May we read and study the Bible more each day as we seek to grow deeper in relationship with you. In Jesus' name, we pray. Amen.

Wednesday, October 25 — Psalm 119:73–80
Ezekiel 29:13–30:26; 1 Peter 1:13–25

All the ends of the earth shall turn to the Lord. Psalm 22:27

All people that on earth do dwell, 539
sing to the Lord with cheerful voice;
serve him with joy, his praises tell,
come now before him and rejoice.

Jesus told them another parable, "The kingdom of heaven is like yeast that a woman took and mixed in with three measures of flour until all of it was leavened." Matthew 13:33

O that Jesus' love and merit 589
filled our hearts both night and day!
May the leading of his Spirit
all our thoughts and actions sway!
Then should we be ever ready
cheerfully to testify
how our spirit, soul and body
do in God our Savior joy.

Good Shepherd, we are people from diverse backgrounds, with varied interests and innumerable ideas. Transform our thinking and lead us away from self-minded activity. Move us, in accordance with the Holy Spirit, to serve you and bolster your church. Amen.

Thursday, October 26 — Psalm 119:81–88
Ezekiel 31:1–32:16; 1 Peter 2:1–12

**He awakens me morning by morning,
he awakens my ear to listen as a disciple.
Isaiah 50:4 NASB**

God, grant me strength to do 615
with ready heart and willing,
whatever you command,
my calling here fulfilling;
and do it when I ought,
with zeal and joyfulness;
and bless the work I've wrought,
for you must give success.

Lydia, a worshiper of God, was listening to us; she was from the city of Thyatira and a dealer in purple cloth. The Lord opened her heart to listen eagerly to what was said by Paul. Acts 16:14

Lord, grant that we impelled by love 643
in smallest things may faithful prove;
till we depart, our lives be true,
devoted wholly unto you.

Thank you, Lord, for the opportunities awaiting us to praise your holy name and witness to your divine love. In our every interaction, may we exemplify our devotion to Jesus Christ by earnestly listening to others and responding with compassion. Amen.

Friday, October 27 — Psalm 119:89–96
Ezekiel 32:17–33:20; 1 Peter 2:13–25

The Lord is the stronghold of my life; of whom shall I be afraid? Psalm 27:1

God is my strong salvation, 769
no enemy I fear;
he hears my supplication,
dispelling all my care;
if he, my head and master,
defend me from above,
what pain or what disaster
can part me from his love?

I can do all things through him who strengthens me. Philippians 4:13

The ground of my profession 769
is Jesus and his blood;
he gives me the possession
of everlasting good.
To me his Holy Spirit
speaks many a precious word
of rest to one who's seeking
a refuge in the Lord.

Resurrected Savior, who instructs us to resist evil, move us this day to disavow notions of power. Teach us to fashion our swords into plowshares, for we are called to be peacemakers. "Christ and Him crucified, remain our confession of faith." Amen.

Saturday, October 28 — Psalm 119:97–104
Ezekiel 33:21–34:19; 1 Peter 3:1–7

Surely it was for my welfare that I had great bitterness; but you have held back my life from the pit of destruction, for you have cast all my sins behind your back. Isaiah 38:17

I need your presence every passing hour. 807
What but your grace can foil the tempter's pow'r?
Who like yourself my guide and strength can be?
Through cloud and sunshine, O abide with me.

By this we will know that we are from the truth and will reassure our hearts before him whenever our hearts condemn us; for God is greater than our hearts, and he knows everything. 1 John 3:19-20

Not the labor of my hands 334r
can fulfill thy law's demands;
could my zeal no respite know,
could my tears forever flow,
all for sin could not atone;
thou must save, and thou alone.

Omniscient God, who makes no mistakes, open our minds and hearts to your mercy. Teach us to accept your grace without questioning your reasoning. Open our eyes, so that we can see ourselves as you see us. Amen.

Twenty-second Sunday after Pentecost

Watchword for the week — You shall be holy, for I the Lord your God am holy. Leviticus 19:2

Sunday, October 29 — Leviticus 19:1-2,15-18; Psalm 1
1 Thessalonians 2:1-8; Matthew 22:34-46

The Lord said, "Whom did you dread and fear so that you lied, and did not remember me?" Isaiah 57:11

What wondrous love is this, 328
O my soul, O my soul!
What wondrous love is this, O my soul!
What wondrous love is this
that caused the Lord of bliss
to bear the dreadful curse for my soul, for my soul,
to bear the dreadful curse for my soul?

You did not receive the spirit of bondage again to fear, but you received the Spirit of adoption by whom we cry out, "Abba, Father." Romans 8:15 NKJV

O then what raptured greetings 394
on Canaan's happy shore;
what knitting severed friendships up,
where partings are no more!
Then eyes with joy shall sparkle
that brimmed with tears of late,
no orphans left without a home,
nor mourners desolate.

Forgive us, Father. Too often we think only of ourselves and become caught up in safeguarding our own interests. On this Sabbath day, let us visit with you. Restore us to right relationship with you. Keep us in the embrace of your holy presence. Amen.

Monday, October 30 — Psalm 119:105–112
Ezekiel 34:20–36:7; 1 Peter 3:8–22

The effect of righteousness will be peace, and the result of righteousness, quietness and trust forever. Isaiah 32:17

Drop thy still dews of quietness, 739
till all our strivings cease.
Take from our souls the strain and stress;
and let our ordered lives confess
the beauty of thy peace.

If you know that Jesus Christ is righteous, you may be sure that everyone who does right has been born of him. 1 John 2:29

To serve the present age, 645
my calling to fulfill,
O may it all my pow'rs engage
to do my Master's will.

Divine Creator, sometimes we wonder about our purpose in life and struggle to make right choices. Forgive us when we lose sight of your most basic truth: you love us just as you made us. Remind us that we are yours and you are ours. In Jesus' name, we pray. Amen.

Tuesday, October 31 — Psalm 119:113–120
Ezekiel 36:8–38; 1 Peter 4

We have all become like one who is unclean and all our righteous deeds are like a filthy cloth. Isaiah 64:6

> Lord, forgive me, day by day, 779
> debts I cannot hope to pay,
> duties I have left undone,
> evils I have failed to shun.

Jesus said, "The son said to him, 'Father, I have sinned against heaven and before you; I am no longer worthy to be called your son.' But the father said to his slaves, 'Quickly, bring out a robe—the best one—and put it on him.'" Luke 15:21-22

> Lord, thy deep humiliation 108r
> has atoned for all my pride;
> I need fear no condemnation,
> since for sinners thou hast died.
> Thou becam'st a curse, dear Savior,
> to restore me to God's favor;
> thousand, thousand thanks to thee,
> dearest Lord, forever be.

We fall short in every way, O Lord. We sin every day. Your mercy, Father, is unbounded, and through the sacrifice of your one and only son, Jesus, you forgive us time and time again. Through your Spirit, empower us to go and sin no more. Amen.

All Saints Day

Watchword for All Saints Day — Salvation belongs to our God who is seated on the throne, and to the Lamb! Revelation 7:10

All Saints Day — Revelation 7:9-17; Psalm 34:1-10,22
1 John 3:1-3; Matthew 5:1-12

Wednesday, November 1 — Psalm 119:121–128
Ezekiel 37:1–38:6; 1 Peter 5

Remember the days of old; consider the generations long past. Ask your father and he will tell you, your elders, and they will explain to you. Deuteronomy 32:7 NIV

All who have gone before us 389*
have shown us how to live
a life of faith and service—
to pray, to praise, to give!
And so as we remember,
more so, we pray that we
may follow their example,
God's ministers to be!

I am reminded of your sincere faith, a faith that lived first in your grandmother Lois and your mother Eunice and now, I am sure, lives in you. 2 Timothy 1:5

May the saints of faith's tomorrow 392**
love and trust the God of grace.
May we grow in hopeful living,
may we know God's strong embrace.
We will still by faith move forward,
till we meet God face to face.

Sustainer God, you care for humanity as a loving parent. We experience your love through the guidance of our faithful elders. Through their example, help us guide, care for, and deeply love those whom our lives touch each day. Amen.

Thursday, November 2 — Psalm 119:129–136
Ezekiel 38:7–39:13; 2 Peter 1:1–11

The Lord God has given me the tongue of disciples, that I may know how to sustain the weary one with a word. Isaiah 50:4 NASB

O teach me, Lord, that I may teach 646
the precious truths which you impart.
And wing my words that they may reach
the hidden depths of many a heart.

When was it that we saw you sick or in prison and visited you? Matthew 25:39

By the Spirit we are gifted 624*
to fulfill Christ's ministry.
With the poor we share our riches,
giving captives liberty.
Hungry, thirsty—we will feed them;
greet the stranger; care and heal;
clothe the naked, free the pris'ner;
serve with gladness and with zeal.

Thank you for empowering each of us to serve and witness, dear Lord. We are grateful for those who have answered the call to ministry, who serve as pastors, teachers, or leaders. May we learn from them that our words and actions will help others come to know you. Amen.

Friday, November 3 — Psalm 119:137–144
Ezekiel 39:14–40:16; 2 Peter 1:12–21

Seek the Lord, all you humble of the land, who do his commands; seek righteousness, seek humility. Zephaniah 2:3

Love is humble, love is gentle, 591*
love is tender, true, and kind;
love is gracious, ever-patient,
generous of heart and mind:
may love be ours, O Lord.

As God's chosen ones, holy and beloved, clothe yourselves with compassion, kindness, humility, meekness, and patience. Colossians 3:12

Never jealous, never selfish, 591*
love will not rejoice in wrong;
never boastful nor resentful,
love believes and suffers long:
may love be ours, O Lord.

Your son, Jesus, taught us how to love unconditionally and serve humbly, dear Lord. May his example guide our thoughts and actions as we patiently, fervently, and graciously care for your children and your earth. Amen.

Saturday, November 4 — Psalm 119:145–152
Ezekiel 40:17–49; 2 Peter 2:1–10

As a mother comforts her child, so I will comfort you. Isaiah 66:13

As a mother feeds her baby, 659
with the milk from her own breast,
giving nourishment and nurture,
loving touch and calming rest,
so God feeds us through communion,
holy presence, blessed food,
loving touch of the Eternal;
hope and wonder are renewed.

Jesus said, "Ask and you will receive, so that your joy may be complete." John 16:24

Called by Christ as friends and learners, 627*
called by Christ for peace on earth,
in this world as Christ's sojourners
we receive new pow'r, new birth.
As we're praising (how amazing!)
we receive new pow'r, new birth.
As we're praising (how amazing!)
we receive new pow'r, new birth.

Sustainer God, often when our lives feel out of control, we seek other sources to comfort us when we should first turn to you. Thank you for the saving grace that has been given to us through your son, Jesus Christ. Our joy is overflowing for your unconditional gift of love. Amen.

Twenty-third Sunday after Pentecost

Watchword for the week — O send out your light and your truth; let them lead me. Psalm 43:3

Sunday, November 5 — Micah 3:5-12; Psalm 43
1 Thessalonians 2:9-13; Matthew 23:1-12

Whoever pursues righteousness and kindness will find life and honor. Proverbs 21:21

O God, my faithful God, 615
O fountain ever flowing,
without whom nothing is,
all perfect gifts bestowing,
grant me a faithful life,
and give me, Lord, within,
commitment free from strife,
a soul unhurt by sin.

Strive first for the kingdom of God and his righteousness, and all these things will be given to you as well. Matthew 6:33

Teacher, Creator, God, 801*
enfold us in your arms;
be with us as we try our wings
and keep us safe from harm.
All good and perfect gifts
come to us from your hand.
O help us use them carefully
and live by love's command.

Each day is a gift from you, gracious God. The air we breathe, the trees that shade our paths, the water that nourishes us—are all gifts from you. Our congregation, our friends and family members, our coworkers, and our pets are blessings that we've received from you. In gratitude for all these gifts and more, let our lives be a blessing to you, to our earth, and to those around us. Amen.

Monday, November 6 — Psalm 119:153–160
Ezekiel 41:1–42:9; 2 Peter 2:11–22

Your way, O God, is holy. Psalm 77:13

God is love; and love enfolds us, 463
all the world in one embrace;
with unfailing grasp God holds us,
ev'ry child of ev'ry race.
And when human hearts are breaking
under sorrow's iron rod,
then we find that self-same aching
deep within the heart of God.

Jesus said, "I came from the Father and have come into the world." John 16:28

The Father's equal, God the Son, 471
with him is ever reigning;
you are partaker of his throne,
and all things are sustaining;
both heaven and earth view their Maker as man,
with joy that is past all expression;
O happy, unspeakably happy, who can
in Jesus find life and salvation.

God of all, since the beginning of time, you have provided for your people. Let us never take you for granted. May we always feel your presence, which upholds us and leads us to eternal life. Amen.

Tuesday, November 7 — Psalm 119:161–168
Ezekiel 42:10–43:21; 2 Peter 3:1–13

I will set up over them one shepherd and he shall feed them. Ezekiel 34:23

As when a shepherd calls his sheep, 417*
they know and heed his voice;
so when you call your fam'ly, Lord,
we follow and rejoice.

When Jesus saw the crowds, he had compassion for them, because they were harassed and helpless, like sheep without a shepherd. Matthew 9:36

Savior, like a shepherd lead us; 731
much we need your tender care;
in your pleasant pastures feed us,
for our use your folds prepare.
Blessed Jesus, blessed Jesus,
you have bought us; yours we are.
Blessed Jesus, blessed Jesus,
you have bought us; yours we are.

Christ our shepherd, lead us. It is so easy to be led astray by the din of the world and combative voices. As a shepherd makes wise decisions for his flock, may we make choices today that advance your way of love and compassionate care for others. Amen.

Wednesday, November 8 — Psalm 119:169–176
Ezekiel 43:22–44:27; 2 Peter 3:14–1 John 1:4

Blessed is the one who comes in the name of the Lord. Psalm 118:26

Praise to the Lord! 530
O, let all that is in me adore him!
All that has life and breath,
come now with praises before him!
Let the amen
sound from his people again.
Gladly forever adore him!

But to all who received him, who believed in his name, he gave power to become children of God. John 1:12

O dear Jesus, you have called us 420*
with your gentle voice;
as your children we receive you
and rejoice.

Through you, Christ, we are joined together with people across our country and around the world; some we know well and many we will never meet. We thank you for this unity and look forward to the day when we will sing your praise together as one. Amen.

Thursday, November 9 — Psalm 120
Ezekiel 44:28–45:25; 1 John 1:5–2:11

I had said in my alarm, "I am driven far from your sight." But you heard my supplications when I cried out to you for help. Psalm 31:22

God, when I stand, no path before me clear, 755*
when ev'ry prayer seems pris'ner of my pain;
come with a gentleness which calms my fear,
Lord of my helplessness, my vict'ry gain.

The Spirit helps us in our weakness; for we do not know how to pray as we ought, but that very Spirit intercedes with sighs too deep for words. Romans 8:26

When all my prayers no answer seem to bring, 755*
and there is silence in my deepest soul;
when in the wilderness I find no spring,
Lord of the desert places, keep me whole.

When our pain and sadness keep us from feeling your light and we hear only silence, we still know that we are not alone. The Spirit is our companion. O Lord of the fertile ground and desert places, thank you for keeping us whole. Amen.

Friday, November 10 — Psalm 121
Ezekiel 46:1–47:12; 1 John 2:12–17

Woe to those who are wise in their own eyes and clever in their own sight. Isaiah 5:21 NIV

We have sinned against your law. 760*
We have failed to do your will,
disobeyed your holy word.
Lord, have mercy on us still.

All of you must clothe yourselves with humility. 1 Peter 5:5

Lord, we your presence seek; 584
we ask this blessing true:
give us a pure and lowly heart,
a temple fit for you.

Compassionate God, forgive us for our self-centeredness and for our love of having many things and amassing more stuff. Help us to live in the world, but not be consumed by its ways. Let all that we do, say, and own be a reflection of our love for you. Amen.

Saturday, November 11 — Psalm 122
Ezekiel 47:13–48:22; 1 John 2:18–29

Jacob went on his way and the angels of God met him. Genesis 32:1

My Father, I have wandered 763*
and hidden from your face;
in foolishness have squandered
your legacy of grace.
But now, in exile dwelling,
I rise with fear and shame,
as distant but compelling,
I hear you call my name.

Are not all angels spirits in the divine service, sent to serve for the sake of those who are to inherit salvation? Hebrews 1:14

Spirit, working in creation, p223**
bringing order out of strife:
Come among God's gathered people,
giving harmony and life.

For the many times that friends and strangers have served as angels in our lives, we thank you, God. Remind us not to be surprised, but to expect that others are moved by the Spirit, and together we can share your light as your gathered people. Amen.

Twenty-fourth Sunday after Pentecost

Watchword for the week — Keep awake therefore, for you know neither the day nor the hour. Matthew 25:13

Sunday, November 12 — Amos 5:18-24; Psalm 70
1 Thessalonians 4:13-18; Matthew 25:1-13

Joseph said to his brothers, "Do not quarrel along the way." Genesis 45:24

Lord, make us servants of your peace: 693*
where there is hate, may we sow love;
where there is hurt, may we forgive;
where there is strife, may we make one.

Bear with one another and, if anyone has a complaint against another, forgive each other; just as the Lord has forgiven you, so you also must forgive. Colossians 3:13

May we not look for love's return, 693*
but seek to love unselfishly,
for in our giving we receive,
and in forgiving are forgiv'n.

Lord, it can be so difficult to forgive after we've been hurt. There is no shortage of stories of people being taken advantage of, done wrong to, or worse. We want justice. We want to know why. Christ has shown us that forgiveness must come first. Spirit, fill us with the strength to forgive, as this is the cornerstone of reconciliation. Amen.

Chief Elder Festival

Chief Elder Festival† — Ezekiel 34:11-16,23-24; Psalm 8
Hebrews 4:14-16; John 10:1-10

Monday, November 13 — Psalm 123
Ezekiel 48:23–Daniel 1:21; 1 John 3:1–10

The Lord God has opened my ear; and I was not disobedient. Nor did I turn back. Isaiah 50:5 NASB

Give deep humility; the sense 750
of godly sorrow give,
a strong desiring confidence
to hear your voice and live.

Jesus said, "They will listen to my voice. So there will be one flock, one shepherd." John 10:16

Join hands, disciples of the faith, 523
whate'er your race may be.
All children of the living God
are surely kin to me.
In Christ shall true hearts ev'rywhere
their high communion find;
his service is the golden cord
close binding humankind.

God, you have given us a story to share with all of humanity. Through your infinite love, you sent your son to bring salvation for all. Christ the shepherd will lead your flock. With Moravians around the world, today we celebrate that Christ is our shepherd and Chief Elder. With eternal gratefulness, we follow his loving example. Amen.

† On this day in 1741, it was announced in all Moravian congregations that Jesus Christ had been chosen Chief Elder of the Moravian Church. The Moravian Church has had no single human chief executive since then, and now observes this is a festival day.

Tuesday, November 14 — Psalm 124
Daniel 2:1–33; 1 John 3:11–24

The Lord said, "I will not continually accuse, nor will I always be angry." Isaiah 57:16

Far as east from west is distant, 458
God has put away our sin;
like the pity of a father
has the Lord's compassion been.

In Christ God was reconciling the world to himself, not counting their trespasses against them, and entrusting the message of reconciliation to us. 2 Corinthians 5:19

Eternal thanks we sing, 488
great author of salvation,
who sinful hearts did bring
to heed your invitation.
We are your property.
O may we yours remain;
this is our only plea,
since you for us were slain.

Forgiving God, we have often fallen short of what you want from us. Thank you for not keeping a tally of those failures and help us extend that grace to our relationships. Strengthen us, so that we can stand firm in your love as challenges confront us today and always. Amen.

Wednesday, November 15 — Psalm 125
Daniel 2:34–3:18; 1 John 4:1–16a

Ho, everyone who thirsts, come to the waters.
Isaiah 55:1

That river flows for all the world, 77s*
and as God's own we are
the means for grace and love to heal
the wounds and mend the scars.
God's love that stirred our church back then,
still moves our church today,
Creator, former, shaper, bringing
new transforming ways.

That evening, at sunset, they brought to him all who were sick or possessed with demons.
Mark 1:32

We praise the Christ who called the rich, 481**
the outcast, and the poor,
who said to them, "Come follow me,
my love for you is sure."
And Christ today invites us still
to follow and to live.
Christ calls us now to spread the news
that God new life does give.

Lord, we are weary travelers. We don't know what lies around the next corner or over the next hill. Thank you for walking with us, side by side. You offer us strength and guidance, particularly when we face our demons. Thank you for your companionship on our journey. Amen.

Thursday, November 16 — Psalm 126
Daniel 3:19–4:18; 1 John 4:16b–5:5

I will make an everlasting covenant with them, never to draw back from doing good to them. Jeremiah 32:40

When we suffer, God sends healing; 534*
when we sin, the Lord forgives;
from the grave the Lord redeems us,
and, by grace, we rise to live!

God's love was revealed among us in this way: God sent his only Son into the world so that we might live through him. 1 John 4:9

God sent his Son, they called him Jesus, 706
he came to love, heal, and forgive;
he lived and died to buy my pardon,
an empty grave is there to prove my Savior lives.

Gracious God, you have called us in covenant to live in harmony with you, with others, and with the world that surrounds us. We know that you will not break this promise, because you sent your son, Jesus, to seal it with his life and death. May we always be faithful to you and forgive us when we falter. Amen.

Friday, November 17 — Psalm 127
Daniel 4:19–5:16; 1 John 5:6–21

My thoughts are not your thoughts, nor are your ways my ways, says the Lord. Isaiah 55:8

"For my thoughts are not like your thoughts," 780*
says the Lord, "nor your ways mine.
Farther still than earth from heaven
are things human from divine."

For God's foolishness is wiser than human wisdom, and God's weakness is stronger than human strength. 1 Corinthians 1:25

Simple innocence, most holy, 715**
forthright, strong, profoundly wise,
shining treasure of the lowly:
God alone this good supplies.

Eternal God, you have always been and will always be. You extend beyond our capacity to comprehend. You chose to fashion us, care for us, and provide for us the opportunity for eternal life through your son, Jesus Christ. Thank you for your love beyond comprehension. Amen.

Saturday, November 18 — Psalm 128
Daniel 5:17–6:18; 2 John

The war horse is a vain hope for victory, and by its great might it cannot save. Truly the eye of the Lord is on those who fear him, on those who hope in his steadfast love. Psalm 33:17-18

I fully am persuaded 769
and joyfully declare
I'm never left unaided,
my Father hears my prayer;
his comforts never fail me,
he stands at my right hand;
when tempests fierce assail me,
they're calm at his command.

We boast in Christ Jesus and have no confidence in the flesh. Philippians 3:3

My hope is built on nothing less 771
than Jesus' blood and righteousness;
no merit of my own I claim
but wholly lean on Jesus' name.

Christ our redeemer, in our hearts, we want to love and serve you. Help us not to be caught up with the temptations of our day, or to let our love for you grow lukewarm. The storms of life often push us into sinking sand. Thank you for not turning away from us. Amen.

Twenty-fifth Sunday after Pentecost

Watchword for the week — So teach us, O God, to count our days that we may gain a wise heart. Psalm 90:12

Sunday, November 19 — Zephaniah 1:7,12-18; Psalm 90:1-8,(9-11),12
1 Thessalonians 5:1-11; Matthew 25:14-30

The lips of a priest should guard knowledge, and people should seek instruction from his mouth, for he is the messenger of the Lord of hosts. Malachi 2:7

May we faithful, may we faithful 636
in our service be,
truly careful, truly careful
in our ministry;
keep us to your church fast bound,
in the faith preserve us sound,
often weeping, often weeping
grateful tears of joy.

Always be prepared to give an answer to everyone who asks you to give the reason for the hope that you have. 1 Peter 3:15 NIV

We are called to be God's prophets, 635*
speaking for the truth and right,
standing firm for godly justice,
bringing evil things to light.
Let us seek the courage needed,
our high calling to fulfill,
that the world may know the blessing
of the doing of God's will.

God, we thank you for those who have accepted your call to serve as leaders of our faith communities. We are grateful for their insights and instruction, and for the humanity they bring to your work here on earth. Help each of us to recognize that we, too, are called to be witnesses to your love to a world in need. Amen.

Monday, November 20 — Psalm 129
Daniel 6:19–7:22; 3 John

Turn, O Lord! How long? Have compassion on your servants! Psalm 90:13

His sov'reign pow'r without our aid 455
formed us of clay and gave us breath;
and when like wand'ring sheep we strayed,
he saved us from the pow'r of death.

Jesus said, "I will come again and will take you to myself, so that where I am, there you may be also." John 14:3

Happy soul, to Christ united, 809*
calmer now and clearer sighted:
your new journey now begins,
freed from earth's besetting sins.
Pressing on towards perfection,
happy soul, happy soul,
happy soul, to Christ united.

Jesus, you are with us in times of distress and fear. Sometimes we don't recognize you or hear your voice, but your steadfast hand is always there. Help us see and hear you and to feel your calming touch. Amen.

Tuesday, November 21 — Psalm 130
Daniel 7:23–8:27; Jude 1:1–10

Thus far the Lord has helped us. 1 Samuel 7:12

The Lord has promised good to me, 783
his word my hope secures;
he will my shield and portion be
as long as life endures.

Paul said, "To this day I have had help from God, and so I stand here, testifying." Acts 26:22

"I'll bless you, 616
and you shall be set for a blessing!"
Thus said God, the Lord, to his servant of old;
O may we, in grace and in number increasing,
through work show our faith and in service be bold;
upon your truth founded, we shall not move,
let us ever follow, and fearless prove;
so shall we in doctrine, in word and behavior,
to ev'ryone witness that Christ is our Savior.

Gracious God, we rejoice in the constant assurance that you are with us. No matter how far we stray, you are always with us. You share our pain and delight in our joys. Today, we will make a point of telling a friend about the strength we receive from your love. What a joy it will be to share. Amen.

Wednesday, November 22 — Psalm 131
Daniel 9:1–10:7; Jude 1:11–25

How can a mortal be just before God? If one wished to contend with him, one could not answer him once in a thousand. Job 9:2-3

Seek the Lord, whose willing presence 780*
moves your heart to make appeal.
Turn from wickedness and evil;
God will pardon, cleanse, and heal.

I will get up and go to my father, and I will say to him, "Father, I have sinned against heaven and before you." Luke 15:18

"Forgive our sins as we forgive," 777**
you taught us, Lord, to pray;
but you alone can grant us grace
to live the words we say,
to live the words we say.

The grace that you have extended to us, dear God, is difficult to comprehend. Your forgiveness of our sins is so radical in a world where people still seek an eye for an eye. Thank you for setting this example, and for being our strength when it is our turn to forgive a wrong done to us. Your grace is life-giving. Amen.

Thursday, November 23 — Psalm 132
Daniel 10:8–11:19; Revelation 1:1–8

God, you know my folly; the wrongs I have done are not hidden from you. Psalm 69:5

O Lord of all the living, 763*
both banished and restored,
compassionate, forgiving
and ever caring Lord,
grant now that my transgressing,
my faithlessness may cease.
Stretch out your hand in blessing,
in pardon and in peace.

In him we have redemption through his blood, the forgiveness of our trespasses, according to the riches of his grace. Ephesians 1:7

All things you send are full of grace; 761**
you crown our lives with favor.
All our good works are done in vain
without our Lord and Savior.
We praise the God who gives us faith
and saves us from the grip of death;
our lives are in his keeping.

Generous God, you have provided every blessing in abundance. As we acknowledge your gifts with thankfulness, we hear your call to share what we have received. And so, we pray that you give us glad and generous hearts and lives that abound in your service. Amen.

Friday, November 24 — Psalm 133
Daniel 11:20–12:7; Revelation 1:9–20

I will say, "They are my people;" and they will say, "The Lord is our God." Zechariah 13:9

> With voices united our praises we offer, 4r
> and gladly our song of true worship we raise;
> our sins now confessing, we pray for thy blessing;
> to thee, our great redeemer, ever be praise!

God will dwell with them; they will be his peoples, and God himself will be with them; he will wipe every tear from their eyes. Revelation 21:3-4

> O God, be near in loneliness and need; 711*
> from fear and doubting may our minds be freed.
> When losses come, your consolation speed;
> for strength and healing love, O Lord, we plead.

Ever-present God, you know our thoughts before we speak and our pain before we cry out. Even in the darkest times, we are not alone, because your Spirit dwells within us. Thank you for holding us in your firm and comforting hand. Amen.

Saturday, November 25 — Psalm 134
Daniel 12:8–Hosea 2:15; Revelation 2:1–11

All that the Lord has spoken we will do, and we will be obedient. Exodus 24:7

> Our reward for the kindness that we show 39s*
> comes from seeing that God's plan will be fulfilled;
> our joy comes from praising God with all our strength,
> so praise the Lord, then do God's will.

But be doers of the word, and not merely hearers who deceive themselves. James 1:22

> Called by Christ to love each other, 627**
> called by Christ to seek the lost,
> may we each, as sister, brother,
> follow Christ, not counting cost.
> One in daring, one in sharing,
> follow Christ, not counting cost.
> One in daring, one in sharing,
> follow Christ, not counting cost.

Lord, you have called us to be doers of the word. Grant us the courage and conviction to love all your children without judgement. Forgive us when we fall short and misrepresent your will. Let us serve you in gladness and find sheer joy in loving others unconditionally. Amen.

Reign of Christ Sunday

Watchword for the week — God said, "I will seek the lost, and I will bring back the strayed, and I will bind up the injured, and I will strengthen the weak." Ezekiel 34:16

Sunday, November 26 — Ezekiel 34:11-16,20-24; Psalm 95:1-7a Ephesians 1:15-23; Matthew 25:31-46

The Lord is good, a stronghold in the day of trouble; and he knows those who trust in him. Nahum 1:7 NKJV

Then let us place ourselves 698*
in God's creative hands,
anchored in faith, but free
to do what God commands:
not pris'ners of our heritage
but born to serve the present age.

Ask, and it will be given you; search, and you will find; knock, and the door will be opened for you. Matthew 7:7

Seek ye first the kingdom of God 605
and his righteousness,
and all these things shall be added unto you—
Allelu, alleluia!

Dear God, through your son, Jesus Christ, you have given us a blueprint for a purposeful life and an invitation to eternal life. Thank you for opening the door when we knock. May our lives reflect our gratitude for your love. May others come to know you through our joy. Amen.

Monday, November 27 — Psalm 135:1–12
Hosea 2:16–4:19; Revelation 2:12–23

Do not oppress the widow, the orphan, the alien, or the poor. Zechariah 7:10

> Today we all are called to be 696*
> disciples of the Lord,
> to help to set the captive free,
> make plowshare out of sword,
> to feed the hungry, quench their thirst,
> make love and peace our fast,
> to serve the poor and homeless first,
> our ease and comfort last.

That is not the way you learned Christ! Ephesians 4:20

> We must not be arrogant, boastful, unkind, 56s**
> but practice compassion and be of one mind.
> May we not be proud of our calling or place,
> but treat all as members of one common race.

Loving Christ, you were the master of doing remarkable acts of kindness—feeding the masses, healing the leper, loving the unlovable. Today, we resolve to reach out to a person we do not know and treat them with kindness in your name. Thank you for letting us know how to express compassion. Amen.

Tuesday, November 28 — Psalm 135:13–21
Hosea 5,6,7; Revelation 2:24–3:6

The unfolding of your words gives light; it imparts understanding to the simple. Psalm 119:130

Called together as God's people, 73s*
finding life we'd just dreamed of,
we are gathered, growing, learning
all the wonders of God's love.
We have found acceptance, meaning;
it's no secret we have grown.
But we can't withhold or hoard it;
we must make the Lord's love known.

For once you were darkness, but now in the Lord you are light. Live as children of light. Ephesians 5:8

God is gracious, God is caring, 73s*
God has shown us how to live.
We find joy and satisfaction
when, like Christ, we learn to give.
We have boldness, strength for action,
when the Spirit's pow'r is shown,
reaching out to others through us,
freely making God's love known.

Gracious God, surrounding me today are countless acts of healing, moments of learning, and opportunities to praise you for the wonders of your creation. We thank you for your wondrous embrace. May we be a light in the lives of others as Christ is the light in ours. Amen.

Wednesday, November 29 — Psalm 136
Hosea 8,9; Revelation 3:7–18

Help, O Lord, for there is no longer anyone who is godly; the faithful have disappeared from humankind. Psalm 12:1

Lord, have mercy upon my soul; 48s*
the war within seems out of control.
Take this bitterness and turn it into gratefulness.
Lord, have mercy upon my soul.

So Jesus asked the twelve, "Do you also wish to go away?" John 6:67

Walk with me each day, Jesus, 45s**
and let my heart be true.
I'll strive to show others
that caring comes from you.
May all whom I encounter
see your love in my face,
and may I be a vessel
of your enduring grace.

Loving God, we can't imagine how you feel when you see us continually hurt each other, tell lies, and discriminate because of gender, race, or economics. Thank you for not turning your back on us. Strengthen us with the Holy Spirit, and, with other faithful ones who know you so well, let us not turn away from taking a stand in your loving name. Amen.

Thursday, November 30 — Psalm 137
Hosea 10,11,12; Revelation 3:19–4:8

For you who revere my name the sun of righteousness shall rise, with healing in its wings. Malachi 4:2

Sun of righteousness, arise; 521*
dawn upon our clouded skies;
shine within your church today
that the world may see and say,
"Have mercy, Lord."

The night is far gone, the day is near. Romans 13:12

Zion hears the watchmen singing, 258
and in her heart new joy is springing.
She wakes, she rises from her gloom.
For her Lord comes down all glorious,
the strong in grace, in truth victorious.
Her star's arising light has come!
"Now come, O blessed one,
Lord Jesus, God's own Son.
Hail, hosanna!
We answer all in joy your call,
we follow to the wedding hall."

You so loved the world, O God, that you sent your son to bring light into the darkness. May we abide in that light, serving as instruments of your transforming love in our homes, our jobs, and our relationships. Amen.

* C. Daniel Crews (1994).

Friday, December 1 — Psalm 138:1–5
Hosea 13,14; Revelation 4:9–5:10

See, I will refine and test my people.
Jeremiah 9:7 NIV

Spirit of God, burst forth in flame, 491*
searing our conscience, staking your claim.
Burn up the clutter, brand us apart;
warm ev'ry recess of my cold heart.

The one who endures to the end will be saved.
Mark 13:13

As you once called two brothers by the sea, 88s**
and you said to these brothers, "Follow me!"
From life's hustle and roar
we have come to this shore.
When you're calling to others, call me.

Enduring and everlasting God, we are your people. As we strive to follow your guidance in all areas of life, help us to pursue your holy will for humankind. Amen.

* © 1980 by David Henkelmann.

** by David M. Henkelmann (1981). © 2013 by IBOC and MMF.

Saturday, December 2 — Psalm 138:6–8
Joel 1:1–2:14; Revelation 5:11–6:8

Be gracious to me, O Lord, for I am in distress. Psalm 31:9

O Lord, hear my prayer, 745
O Lord, hear my prayer:
when I call answer me.
O Lord, hear my prayer,
O Lord, hear my prayer.
Come and listen to me.

His disciples awoke Jesus, saying, "Lord, save us! We are perishing!" But he said to them, "Why are you fearful, O you of little faith?" Then he arose and rebuked the winds and the sea, and there was a great calm. Matthew 8:25-26 NKJV

As you once calmed a storm on the sea, 88s*
and you spoke words of "Peace! Let it be!"
In my raging and doubt,
fears within and without,
as you once calmed that storm, calm me.

O Lord of sea and sky, calm our fears and grant to us a quiet spirit. As we transition from one season to another, let us find comfort in these words of hope and promise. Restore our faith. Amen.

* by David M. Henkelmann (1981).

First Sunday in Advent

Watchword for the week — Then they will see 'the Son of Man coming in clouds' with great power and glory. Mark 13:26

Sunday, December 3 — Isaiah 64:1-9; Psalm 80:1-7,17-19
1 Corinthians 1:3-9; Mark 13:24-37

The Lord will again comfort Zion. Zechariah 1:17

"Comfort, comfort now my people; 264
tell of peace!" So says our God.
Comfort those who sit in darkness
bowed beneath oppression's load.
To God's people now proclaim
that God's pardon waits for them!
Tell them that their war is over;
God will reign in peace forever!

Simeon was looking forward to the consolation of Israel, and the Holy Spirit rested on him. Luke 2:25

As prophets in the temple knew, 28s*
you came to light our way.
As wise men gave, we give to you
heart, mind, and strength today.

O promise-keeping God, through prophets and patriarchs, we hear the good news of salvation and restoration. May your spirit rest upon us in these days of Advent. In your name, we pray. Amen.

Monday, December 4 — Psalm 139:1–6
Joel 2:15–3:21; Revelation 6:9–7:17

Do not fear, for I am with you; do not be afraid, for I am your God. Isaiah 41:10 NIV

"Fear not, I am with you; O be not dismayed, 709
for I am your God and will still give you aid;
I'll strengthen you, help you and cause you to stand
upheld by my righteous, omnipotent hand."

The children were crying out in the temple, "Hosanna to the Son of David." Matthew 21:15

All glory, laud, and honor 342
to you, Redeemer, King,
to whom the lips of children
made sweet hosannas ring.
You are the King of Israel
and David's royal Son,
now in the Lord's name coming,
the king and Blessed One.

O God of children who sang prophetic praises in the streets long ago, amplify our voices into one resounding song of glory and promise in our days. Never let us forget your comforting presence as we journey through the week. We pray this, in Jesus' name. Amen.

Tuesday, December 5 — Psalm 139:7–12
Amos 1,2,3; Revelation 8

When deeds of iniquity overwhelm us, you forgive our transgressions. Psalm 65:3

Forgive me, Lord, for this I pray, 569
the wrong that I have done this day.
May peace with God and neighbor be,
before I sleep, restored to me.

When the fullness of time had come, God sent his Son, born of a woman, born under the law, in order to redeem those who were under the law, so that we might receive adoption as children. Galatians 4:4-5

O Savior, child of Mary, 302*
who felt all human woe;
O Savior, king of glory,
who triumphed o'er our foe:
bring us at length, we pray,
to the bright courts of heaven
and into endless day.

Forgiving Creator, we are humbled to see your great promise fulfilled in the birth of Jesus, the Christ. Forgive us of our sins as we grow in grace; bless us with grateful hearts and a new identity as children of God. Amen.

Wednesday, December 6 — Psalm 139:13–16
Amos 4,5; Revelation 9:1–11

Your days of mourning shall be ended. Isaiah 60:20

God is waiting for us all 57s*
to wake up from our sleep.
If we'd only hear the call
such love we would receive.

The Word became flesh and lived among us, and we have seen his glory, the glory as of a father's only son, full of grace and truth. John 1:14

The Christ Child is not far away. 37s**
The manger's here to see,
for sages and for shepherds too;
he's born for you and me.
If Christmas is to live for you,
then look and see the star
above the heads of those around,
of neighbors near and far.

Mysterious and majestic God, we long for the coming of Jesus, our Lord, with grace and glory. May your divine word live in our hearts, so that we may bear witness to your love for the entire world. Amen.

Thursday, December 7 — Psalm 139:17–24
Amos 6,7; Revelation 9:12–21

The Israelites cried to the Lord, saying, "We have sinned against you, because we have abandoned our God." Judges 10:10

God forgives all your transgressions, 458
all diseases gently heals,
God redeems you from destruction,
and with you so kindly deals.

Zechariah said, "You will go before the Lord to prepare his ways, to give knowledge of salvation to his people by the forgiveness of their sins." Luke 1:76-77

O come, O wisdom from on high, 274
and order all things far and nigh;
to us the path of knowledge show,
and teach us in her ways to go.

O Holy One, ageless and forgiving, timeless and loving, we bow before you confessing our unrighteousness. We humbly ask that you restore us to a place of favor in your sight. In the name of Jesus, we pray. Amen.

Friday, December 8 — Psalm 140:1–5
Amos 8,9; Revelation 10

Do not remember the former things, or consider the things of old. I am about to do a new thing; now it springs forth, do you not perceive it? Isaiah 43:18-19

New songs of celebration render 545*
to God who has great wonders done;
awed by his love his foes surrender
and fall before the Mighty One.
He has made known his great salvation
which all his friends with joy confess;
he has revealed to ev'ry nation
his everlasting righteousness.

The kingdom of heaven is like a mustard seed that someone took and sowed in his field. Matthew 13:31

Like a tiny seed of mustard, 702**
stored with life, invisibly,
grows and grows, each day increasing
and becomes a mighty tree;

Like a gardener, O God, you plant seeds of hope in our world even when we do not perceive your work among us. As we prepare ourselves during this season of hope, give us a renewed sense of gratitude for your kingdom which is always unfolding. Amen.

Saturday, December 9 — Psalm 140:6–13
Obadiah 1; Jonah 1,2; Revelation 11:1–14

You, Lord, brought me up from the realm of the dead; you spared me from going down to the pit. Psalm 30:3 NIV

So shall my walk be close with God, 747*
my wand'rings be forgiv'n;
so shall his light mark out the road
that leads at last to heav'n.

Jesus said, "The hour is coming, and is now here, when the dead will hear the voice of the Son of God, and those who hear will live." John 5:25

Sleep thy last sleep, 805
free from care and sorrow;
rest, where none weep,
till the eternal morrow;
though dark waves roll
o'er the silent river,
thy fainting soul
Jesus can deliver.

O God, death is not the end to those who love you. Thank you for the gift of life eternal as we confess our faith in you, our redeemer, friend, and savior. Amen.

Second Sunday in Advent

Watchword for the week — He will feed his flock like a shepherd; he will gather the lambs in his arms, and carry them in his bosom. Isaiah 40:11

Sunday, December 10 — Isaiah 40:1-11; Psalm 85:1-2,8-13
2 Peter 3:8-15a; Mark 1:1-8

What god in heaven or on earth can perform deeds and mighty acts like yours! Deuteronomy 3:24

Great Father of glory, pure Father of light, 457
your angels adore you, all veiling their sight;
all praise we would render, O lead us to see
the light of your splendor, your love's majesty.

There are different kinds of working, but in all of them and in everyone it is the same God at work. 1 Corinthians 12:6 NIV

Praise and glory, Holy Spirit, p223*
for your love on us out-poured,
giving honor to the Father
and proclaiming Jesus "Lord."

O divine Master, how great are you in all your works. Let your spirit fill our lives with gifts of power and purpose, so that your kingdom may prosper and fulfill your design. Amen.

Monday, December 11 — Psalm 141:1–4
Jonah 3,4; Revelation 11:15–12:6

O Lord, all my longing is known to you; my sighing is not hidden from you. Psalm 38:9

God his own shall tend and nourish, 667*
in his holy courts they flourish.
From all evil pow'rs he spares them;
in his mighty arms he bears them.

And this is the boldness we have in him, that if we ask anything according to his will, he hears us. 1 John 5:14

Have we trials and temptations? 743
Is there trouble anywhere?
We should never be discouraged;
take it to the Lord in prayer!
Can we find a friend so faithful
who will all our sorrows share?
Jesus knows our ev'ry weakness;
take it to the Lord in prayer!

Healer of the nations, speak to our hearts this day as we consider the challenges and concerns of our lives. Sustain us with your spirit in all our endeavors this week. In your name, we pray. Amen.

Tuesday, December 12 — Psalm 141:5–10
Micah 1– 3:7; Revelation 12:7–18

God blessed the seventh day and hallowed it, because on it God rested from all the work that he had done. Genesis 2:3

This is my Father's world: 456
he shines in all that's fair;
in rustling grass I hear him pass—
he speaks to me ev'rywhere.
This is my Father's world:
why should my heart be sad?
The Lord is King, let heaven ring!
God reigns; let earth be glad.

And the peace of God, which surpasses all understanding, will guard your hearts and your minds in Christ Jesus. Philippians 4:7

I've got peace like a river, 592
I've got peace like a river,
I've got peace like a river in my soul,
I've got peace like a river,
I've got peace like a river,
I've got peace like a river in my soul.

Lord of creation, may we find sabbath rest in all our activities—work, leisure, tasks, and obligations. In this complex world in which we live, give us peace. Thank you, Lord. Amen.

Wednesday, December 13 — Psalm 142
Micah 3:8–5:15; Revelation 12:19–13:10

Even before a word is on my tongue, O Lord, you know it completely. Psalm 139:4

Let holy thoughts be ours 575
when sleep o'ertakes us;
our earliest thoughts be yours
when morning wakes us;
for your dear presence will not leave those lonely
who seek you only.

The Lord will bring to light what is hidden in darkness and will expose the motives of the heart. 1 Corinthians 4:5 NIV

Light of light, we humbly pray, 276*
shine upon your world today;
break the gloom of our dark night,
fill our souls with love and light,
give your blessed word rebirth,
"Peace, good will to all on earth."

Merciful God, in the assurance of your grace, we confess our sins and seek your guidance in both the light and dark moments of our lives. May your light bring us hope and restoration in our daily living. In your name, we pray. Amen.

Thursday, December 14 — Psalm 143:1–6
Micah 6,7; Revelation 13:11–14:5

Light dawns for the righteous, and joy for the upright in heart. Psalm 97:11

Light of the world, we worship you; p68
our gifts to you we bring;
accept our sinful hearts, O Lord,
while praise to you we sing.

Jesus said, "Then the kingdom of heaven will be like this: Ten bridesmaids took their lamps and went to meet the bridegroom. Five of them were foolish, and five were wise." Matthew 25:1-2

The watchers on the mountain 256
proclaim the bridegroom near;
go forth as he approaches
with alleluias clear.
The marriage feast is waiting;
the gates wide open stand.
Arise, O heirs of glory;
the bridegroom is at hand.

Keeper of promises, gather us to your bosom as we seek refuge from the challenges around us. As wise servants in your kingdom, let us choose peace, hope, and love. In your name, we pray. Amen.

Friday, December 15 — Psalm 143:7–12
Nahum 1,2; Revelation 14:6–16

Some went down to the sea in ships, and saw the deeds of the Lord, his wondrous works in the deep. Let them thank the Lord for his steadfast love, for his wonderful works to humankind. Psalm 107:23,24,31

I search for you, Lord, 90s*
in the washing and churching of ocean's tide.
I look for your presence
in all the brightness of morning's sky.
I wander in fields of clover and flowers
that smell so sweet.
I feel the brown earth and soft grass under my feet.

After we had reached safety, we then learned that the island was called Malta. The natives showed us unusual kindness. They kindled a fire and welcomed all of us around it. Acts 28:1-2

Make it known to folks among us. 73s**
Do it now, this very hour.
Let us listen, love and serve them,
acting in the Spirit's pow'r.
Make it known to those outside us,
where the seed of faith is sown.
We will pray and work together
as we make the Lord's love known.

Welcoming Creator, we thank you for your hospitality and provisions for all of us. In our daily work, may we be kind to others, and so become ambassadors of your royal law. Amen.

* by Rick Sides and Jim Newsom, Jr. (1974). © 2013 IBOC and MMF.

** © 1993 by Darryl Bell.

Saturday, December 16 — Psalm 144:1–4
Nahum 3; Habakkuk 1; Revelation 14:17–15:8

In response to his people the Lord said, "I am sending you grain, wine, and oil, and you will be satisfied." Joel 2:19

For the fruit of all creation, 449*
thanks be to God.
For his gifts to ev'ry nation,
thanks be to God.
For the plowing, sowing, reaping,
silent growth while we are sleeping,
future needs in earth's safekeeping,
thanks be to God.

Taking the five loaves and the two fish, Jesus looked up to heaven, and blessed and broke the loaves, and gave them to the disciples, and the disciples gave them to the crowds. And all ate and were filled. Matthew 14:19-20

As you once fed your friends by the sea, 88s**
and you said, "Come, break bread with me,"
though I eat my full share, still a hunger is there.
I need more, O my Lord, feed me.

Through your sustaining spirit, we are fed with good provisions for all of us, O Lord. As people of faith, let us share the abundance of God's provisions with those in need. Thank you, God. Amen.

Third Sunday in Advent

Watchword for the week — May the God of peace sanctify you entirely; and may your spirit and soul and body be kept sound and blameless at the coming of our Lord Jesus Christ. 1 Thessalonians 5:23

Sunday, December 17 — Isaiah 61:1-4, 8-11; Psalm 126
1 Thessalonians 5:16-24; John 1:6-8,19-28

God is not a human being, that he should lie, or a mortal, that he should change his mind. Numbers 23:19

Holy, holy, holy! Though the darkness hide thee, 381
though the eye made blind by sin
thy glory may not see,
only thou art holy; there is none beside thee,
perfect in pow'r, in love, and purity.

As surely as God is faithful, our word to you has not been "Yes and No." For the Son of God, Jesus Christ, whom we proclaimed among you, Silvanus and Timothy and I, was not "Yes and No"; but in him it is always "Yes." 2 Corinthians 1:18-19

Whatever God ordains is right; 718*
all that he does is for us.
He heals our souls and gives us sight
and puts no ill before us.
Our God is true; he makes us new;
our lives are built upon his rock,
our cornerstone and building block.

Sustaining Provider, our faith is firmly placed in your divine "Yes." May this Advent season be filled with the realization of your majestic presence in all that we ask or hope for in this life. In Jesus' name, we pray. Amen.

Monday, December 18 — Psalm 144:5–8
Habakkuk 2,3; Revelation 16:1–11

He changes times and seasons, deposes kings and sets up kings. Daniel 2:21

Before the Lord's eternal throne, 455
you nations, bow with sacred joy;
know that the Lord is God alone;
he can create, and he destroy.

He has brought down the powerful from their thrones, and lifted up the lowly. Luke 1:52

Prophesied in days of old, alleluia! 303
God has sent him as foretold, alleluia!
Of a virgin lowly,
he the king most holy,
born this day to save us.

O God, like Mary, we sense the coming kingdom as one that confounds even the wise and powerful. As we continue this Advent journey, keep us focused on your eternal kingdom. Amen.

Tuesday, December 19 — Psalm 144:9–15
Zephaniah 1,2; Revelation 16:12–21

The eyes of the Lord are on the righteous, and his ears are open to their cry. Psalm 34:15

Open then our hearts and senses 684*
to your Spirit's varied ways.
Overcome our self-defenses
so we hear the prayer and praise
which the folk of countless cultures
in new words and rhythms raise.

Rejoice in hope, be patient in suffering, persevere in prayer. Romans 12:12

When we seek relief 799
from a long-felt grief,
when temptations come alluring,
make us patient and enduring;
show us that bright shore
where we weep no more.

Lord God of healing, let us find our wholeness in your constant provisions of deep concern and compassion for all your children. In your name, we pray. Amen.

* Ted Wilde (1984). Used by permission.

Wednesday, December 20 — Psalm 145:1–7
Zephaniah 3; Haggai 1; Revelation 17:1–8

Bless the Lord, who forgives all your iniquity, who heals all your diseases. Psalm 103:2,3

Forgive me, Lord, where I have erred 686*
by loveless act and thoughtless word.
Break down the wall that would divide
your children, Lord, on ev'ry side.

In this is love, not that we loved God but that he loved us and sent his Son to be the atoning sacrifice for our sins. 1 John 4:10

Love divine, all loves excelling, 474
joy of heav'n, to earth come down!
Fix in us your humble dwelling,
all your faithful mercies crown.
Jesus, you are all compassion,
pure, unbounded love impart!
Visit us with your salvation,
enter ev'ry trembling heart.

Forgiving God, as we confess our sins, restore us and renew our devotion to you. Thank you for the gift of your son, Jesus Christ, who forgives sin daily and abundantly. Amen.

Thursday, December 21 — Psalm 145:8–16
Haggai 2; Revelation 17:9–18

I will put my Spirit in you and you will live, and I will settle you in your own land. Then you will know that I the Lord have spoken, and I have done it. Ezekiel 37:14 NIV

When we lift our pack and go, 793*
when we seek another country,
moving far from all we know,
when we long to journey free—
God is in the other place,
God is in another's face,
in the faith we travel by,
God is in the other place.

Where the Spirit of the Lord is, there is freedom. 2 Corinthians 3:17

Candle glowing, my heart knowing 63s**
I should follow him;
Jesus leading, guiding, pleading,
let no light be dim.

O Lord of ancient lands and places, let your Spirit rest upon us. Help us to claim your promises of freedom and new life in your heavenly kingdom. In your name, we pray. Amen.

Friday, December 22 — Psalm 145:17–21
Zechariah 1,2; Revelation 18:1–10

If you will not listen to the voice of the Lord, then the hand of the Lord will be against you, as it was against your fathers. 1 Samuel 12:15 NASB

Be still, my soul: the hour is hast'ning on 757
when we shall be forever with the Lord,
when disappointment, grief, and fear are gone,
sorrow forgot, love's purest joys restored.
Be still, my soul: when change and tears are past,
all safe and blessed we shall meet at last.

But those who look into the perfect law, the law of liberty, and persevere, being not hearers who forget but doers who act—they will be blessed in their doing. James 1:25

Lest the gifts we offer, 651*
money, talents, time,
serve to salve our conscience,
to our secret shame:
Lord, reprove, inspire us
by the way you give;
teach us, dying Savior,
how true Christians live.

Remembering God, throughout the ages, you have led your people in times of disobedience and obedience. As we observe your law, help us to choose wisely in all our actions. Amen.

Saturday, December 23 — Psalm 146
Zechariah 3–5; Revelation 18:11–24

The Lord said, "I desire steadfast love and not sacrifice, the knowledge of God rather than burnt-offerings." Hosea 6:6

I will seek God's help in all my life; 51s*
to follow the way in calm or strife;
to flourish in faith with God as guide:
enfolded in love I will abide.

Therefore, love is the fulfilling of the law. Romans 13:10

This love of God and self and 58s**
all reflects divinity.
It is the essence of God's law to guide humanity.

Most holy God, let us love not only in word and deed, but in our devotion to you. In the deepest part of our being, instill within us the truth of your constant love for all people. In your name, we pray. Amen.

Fourth Sunday in Advent

Watchword for the week — The Mighty One has done great things for me, and holy is his name. Luke 1:49

Sunday, December 24 — 2 Samuel 7:1-11,16; Luke 1:47-55
Romans 16:25-27; Luke 1:26-38

For darkness shall cover the earth, and thick darkness the peoples; but the Lord will arise upon you, and his glory will appear over you. Isaiah 60:2

Lord of all being, throned afar, 464
your glory flames from sun and star;
center and soul of ev'ry sphere,
yet to each loving heart how near!

When the angels had left them and gone into heaven, the shepherds said to one another, "Let us go now to Bethlehem and see this thing that has taken place, which the Lord has made known to us." Luke 2:15

Come with the gladsome shepherds, 284
quick hast'ning from the fold;
come with the wise men, pouring
incense and myrrh and gold.
Come to him, poor and lowly,
around the cradle throng,
come with your hearts of sunshine,
and sing the angels' song.

With excitement, great God, we, like the shepherds, look for your glory to be revealed in the birth of Jesus. May our proclamation be filled with joy and promise. Come Lord Jesus, come. Amen.

Nativity of the Lord (Christmas)

Watchword for the Nativity — Jesus is the reflection of God's glory and the exact imprint of God's very being, and he sustains all things by his powerful word. Hebrews 1:3

Nativity of the Lord (Christmas) — Isaiah 52:7-10; Psalm 98
Hebrews 1:1-4,(5-12); John 1:1-14

Monday, December 25 — Psalm 147:1–6
Zechariah 6,7; Revelation 19:1–8

O Lord, I am oppressed; be my security! Isaiah 38:14

Now let all the heav'ns adore you, 258
let saints and angels sing before you
with harp and cymbal's clearest tone.
Of one pearl each shining portal,
where, joining with the choir immortal,
we gather round your radiant throne.
No eye has seen that light,
no ear the echoed might
of your glory;
yet there shall we in your vict'ry
sing shouts of praise eternally!

To you is born this day a Savior. Luke 2:11

Christ the Lord to us is born, alleluia! 303
On this joyous Christmas morn, alleluia!
Of a virgin lowly,
he the king most holy,
born this day to save us.

Today, we celebrate in our homes and churches; we rejoice in the Savior's birth. Let our focus today be on the word that was made flesh, our Lord, Jesus Christ. We give thanks to God for this most wonderful gift today. Amen.

Tuesday, December 26 — Psalm 147:7–14
Zechariah 8,9; Revelation 19:9–21

I, the Lord, am your Savior and your Redeemer, the Mighty One. Isaiah 60:16

Lifegiving Creator of both great and small; 457
of all life the maker, the true life of all;
we blossom, then wither like leaves on the tree,
but you live forever who was and will be.

It has now been revealed through the appearing of our Savior Christ Jesus, who abolished death and brought life and immortality to light through the gospel. 2 Timothy 1:10

You are the Son of God, 35s*
the Savior of humankind,
you are the light of the world.
Open our hearts, dear Jesus,
fill us deep inside,
under the glow of that star up in the sky.

Lord God, revealed in Jesus, the closing days of a year provide for us a time of reflection. As we conclude the year, let us give thanks for the gifts of life, hope, and abundant joy that overcome death! Amen.

Wednesday, December 27 — Psalm 147:15–20
Zechariah 10,11; Revelation 20:1–10

I am the first and I am the last; besides me there is no god. Isaiah 44:6

Hail, First and Last, the great I Am, 703
in whom we live and move;
increase our little spark of faith,
and fill our hearts with love.

Pray then in this way: Our Father in heaven, hallowed be your name. Matthew 6:9

In the morning when I rise, 573
in the morning when I rise,
in the morning when I rise,
give me Jesus.

Our Father in heaven, with our whole being we worship you. In your name, we offer our petitions and supplications. In the assurance of your great mercy and love, lead us forward with courage. Amen.

Thursday, December 28 — Psalm 148:1–6
Zechariah 12,13; Revelation 20:11–21:8

You cause the grass to grow for the cattle, and plants for people to use, to bring forth food from the earth. Psalm 104:14

Love of God is a fragrant garden, 83s*
full of color, life and fruit.
Throughout its annual cycle,
we find seed and bulb and shoot.
Hiding under the snows of winter,
soaking up the rain of spring,
bathing in the gold of summer,
they an autumn harvest bring.

Give thanks to God the Father at all times and for everything in the name of our Lord Jesus Christ. Ephesians 5:20

Give thanks in hope, rejoice, repent, 451**
and practice all you prayed;
true thanks can never be content
to foul the world God made.

Creator of all things, as the world changes and seasons come and go, we reflect on your artistry in all of creation. We give thanks for the blessings of this beautiful, complex world. Amen.

Friday, December 29 — Psalm 148:7–14
Zechariah 14-Malachi 1; Revelation 21:9–27

When you return to the Lord your God, then the Lord your God will restore you from captivity, and have compassion on you. Deuteronomy 30:2,3 NASB

My God will lead me to a spot 794
where, all my cares and griefs forgot,
I shall enjoy sweet rest.
As pants for cooling streams the hart,
I languish for my heavenly part,
for God, for God, my Refuge blessed.

The time is fulfilled, and the kingdom of God has come near; repent, and believe in the good news. Mark 1:15

Renew this world you made, 674*
our study, work and rest.
In Christ your Son, we rise restored;
in him, our homes are blessed.

Merciful God, we confess our shortcomings and stubbornness in our behavior and actions. Help us to conform to your will in our thoughts and how we live. In your name, we pray. Amen.

Saturday, December 30 — Psalm 149-150
Malachi 2-4; Revelation 22

Joseph said to his master's wife, who tried to seduce him, "How then could I do this great wickedness, and sin against God?" Genesis 39:9

We learn through families 678*
how our closeness and trust
increase when our actions are loving and just.
Yet families have also distorted their roles,
mistreating their members and bruising their souls.

For God did not call us to be impure, but to live a holy life. 1 Thessalonians 4:7 NIV

Won't you walk with me, Jesus, 87s**
down the long road of life?
Won't you walk with me, Jesus all the way?
I keep seeing you in others,
in my sisters, in my brothers;
help me reach out, O Jesus, on my way.

Lord God, we are often careless in our interactions with those around us. Cleanse our hearts from impurity and corruptness. Restore us to new life and keep us on the path to right living. Amen.

First Sunday after Christmas

Watchword for the week — But when the fullness of time had come, God sent his Son, born of a woman, born under the law, in order to redeem those who were under the law, so that we might receive adoption as children. Galatians 4:4,5

Sunday, December 31 — Isaiah 61:10-62:3; Psalm 148
Galatians 4:4-7; Luke 2:22-40

For a brief moment I abandoned you, but with great compassion I will gather you. Isaiah 54:7

Children of the heav'nly Father 667*
safely in his bosom gather;
nestling bird nor star in heaven
such a refuge e'er was given.

Now may our Lord Jesus Christ himself and God our Father, who loved us and through grace gave us eternal comfort and good hope, comfort your hearts and strengthen them in every good work and word. 2 Thessalonians 2:16-17

Let us follow our Lamb 79s**
to the hillsides and shores
where the hungry sit list'ning and thirsting for more
of Christ's life-giving water and loaves we provide,
trusting Jesus to coach us and walk by our side.

Gentle Savior, gracious God, and loving Spirit, you are consistent in your dealings with your children. As you gather us together in worship this day, let us renew our covenant with you. Bless us, O Lord, and help us to grow in grace this day. Amen.

Die Losungen für Sie

Unser vielfältiges Losungsangebot

Die Losungen der Herrnhuter Brüdergemeine erscheinen in verschiedenen Ausgaben. So kann jeder täglich den guten Gedanken Gottes in der Form erfahren, die ihm am meisten zusagt. Eines haben alle Losungsausgaben gemeinsam: Sie setzen Glaubensakzente in unserem Alltag! Folgendes Losungsangebot erhalten Sie im Buchhandel oder unter diesen Adressen:

Losungen in Deutsch, Englisch, Französisch und Spanisch und Ursprache (Altgriechisch/Hebräisch) erhalten Sie in der Comenius-Buchhandlung Herrnhut, der Buchhandlung der Brüder-Unität.

Comenius-Buchhandlung
Comeniusstr. 2, D-02747 Herrnhut
Telefon +49 (0) 3 58 73/22 53
E-Mail comeniusbuchhandlung@herrnhuter-sterne.de
www.comeniusbuchhandlung.de

Weitere Sprachen können Sie bestellen bei der

Evangelische Brüder-Unität
Sebastian Faber
Zittauer Str. 20, D-02747 Herrnhut
Telefon +49 (0) 3 58 73/487 28
E-Mail fremdsprachen@ebu.de
www.losungen.de

Losungen in Blindenschrift und zum Hören
Dachverband der ev. Blinden- und
ev. Sehbehindertenseelsorge (DeBeSS)
Pfarrerin Barbara Brusius
Ständeplatz 18, D-34117 Kassel
Telefon +49 (0) 5 61/72 98 71 61
E-Mail buero@debess.de
www.debess.de

Losungen für Gehörlose
Gehörlosenseelsorge in der Evangelischen Kirche von Westfalen
Pfarrer Christian Schröder
Tonweg 23, D-32429 Minden
Telefon +49 (0) 5 71/648 11 06
E-Mail Schroeder@gebaerdenkreuz.de

Informationen zum Sortiment finden Sie umseitig und im Internet unter www.losungen.de

Deutsche Ausgaben

Normalausgabe, kartoniert	5,90 EUR
Normalausgabe, Geschenkausgabe	6,80 EUR
Losungen für junge Leute	12,80 EUR
Großdruckausgabe, kartoniert	6,90 EUR
Großdruckausgabe, gebunden	8,50 EUR
Großdruckausgabe, Geschenkausgabe	7,90 EUR
Schreibausgabe, gebunden	9,95 EUR
Terminkalender mit Losungen	9,60 EUR
Losungsprogramm für alle Windows-Versionen (inkl. 64Bit) ab Windows 98 bis Win 10	11,70 EUR
Losungs-Box mit 365 Spruchkarten	13,90 EUR
Losungs-Box, Nachfüllpackung	11,20 EUR
Abreißkalender	9,90 EUR
Licht und Kraft (Losungen mit Auslegung)	
Reiseausgabe	14,80 EUR
Gebundene Ausgabe	15,80 EUR

weitere Ausgaben

Moravian Daily Texts, engl. Ausgabe	9,95 EUR
Paroles et Textes, franz. Ausgabe	7,40 EUR
Lecturas Diarias, span. Ausgabe	7,40 EUR
Losungen in der Ursprache	16,95 EUR

Bitte informieren Sie sich zur Losungs-App unter www.losungen.de.